80. thread
71. color

NOTHING-BETTER-THAN

My loving and lovable family:

Mark, Janet, & Lauryn
Peter, Louise, & Emma

———————————

My companions in learning
the writer's craft:

Sharon Clare
Sheila Tucker
Carole-Ann Vance
Donna Langevin

Something-Other-Than

Small joys can come from the dog
who jumps over the sun and falls
into a fiery ball at your feet
where he shakes the ashes
off his fur, licks your hand
and takes you for a walk.

Linda Cassidy

For most of her long, rich life, Linda Cassidy has yearned to discover *the password to the invisible, glorious universe … that cracks the mystery of human existence.* Appreciative of, yet never affiliated with any traditional religion, she has instead travelled other paths to attain an understanding of the universe, through the way of books, yoga, poetry, and the cosmos. Eloquent yet accessible, humorous and poignant, this wide-ranging memoir may not arrive at the ultimate *holy bolt of revelation.* However, the *jewels of deep understanding* garnered along her journey, will surprise and delight her co-travelers.

Donna Langevin, poet/playwright
Author of *Timed Radiance* and *A Story for Sadie*

Something-Other-Than

A Spiritual Memoir

BY

LINDA CASSIDY

Anchusa
Books

Anchusa Books

(http://lindacassidy.ca)

FriesenPress

One Printers Way
Altona, MB R0G 0B0
Canada

www.friesenpress.com

ISBN
978-1-03-917508-2 (Hardcover)
978-1-03-917507-5 (Paperback)
978-1-03-917509-9 (eBook)

1. Body, Mind & Spirit, Inspiration & Personal Growth

Distributed to the trade by The Ingram Book Company

CONTENTS

PREFACE

For a significant portion of my life, I've yearned for something that I could not name—a secret knowledge shared by others but for some reason unknown to me. If I searched hard and long enough, so my thinking went, I might discover the password to this invisible, glorious universe I chose to call "Something-Other-Than." While the phrase is rather vague, it creates in my mind a spaciousness for whatever I might find on my quest, without being restricted by traditional theologies formulated by others.

I'm under no illusion of being the only one to experience such a yearning. For millennia philosophers, mystics, poets, and psychologists have tried to crack the mystery of human existence. The great religions of Christianity, Islam, Judaism, and Hinduism have spent centuries honing the results of their pursuit of this craving, claiming to have had direct conversations with God about the divine order of the world and the way to behave in daily life so as to reap His heavenly reward. Prophets, priests, and ordained ministers have devoted their lives to writing sacred texts about these revelations, in the process establishing ecclesiastic hierarchies, grand buildings, and complex rituals to help seekers navigate the razor's edge of the holy lifestyle. Those raised within these established religions would, I'm sure, see my lone quest for an answer as an act of supreme hubris. Who am I to think I can discover a wisdom on my own that the venerated prophets were unable to find?

In return, I ask why should something so essential as our divine nature be kept a dark secret, open only to the chosen few? Why is it not possible for a person to penetrate life's mystery without relying on intermediaries to dictate the answers? Over the centuries billions of people around the world have adhered to the instructions of religious creeds drawn up thousands of years ago, to the point of performing horrendous deeds well outside the guidelines of the founding sacred texts. A gap exists between the founders of a religion who had a direct experience of the divine and the varied interpretations over the centuries which have distorted the enlightened message of that long-ago prophet or deity.

I wasn't raised within the comfort and confines of a traditional religious community. Some might say I was religiously malnourished as a child, although I've always considered this so-called lack in my upbringing as a great source of freedom, one that liberated me from conformance to religious rules and conceptions drawn up by others and lacking accessible evidence. I was able to freely explore the possibilities of experiencing the divine without being devoured by guilt and a fear of being assigned to eternal damnation.

This memoir recounts how I navigated my spiritual quest using approaches available to any seeker trying to figure out the purpose of this confounding situation we call "Life," and what happens when we arrive at its endpoint. I've focused on five ways: the Way of the Book, the Way of Yoga, the Way of Poetry, the Way of the Dream, and the Way of the Cosmos. To be sure, there are many other ways to divine enlightenment, but only so many can be undertaken within the span of one human lifetime. Heading into my eighth decade, I want to share my experiences of this quest and what it taught me about the mystical world of Something-Other-Than.

We rarely speak of our experiences of the divine, fearing to open ourselves to ridicule. I believe a willingness for each of us to express our discovered truths, while honouring the truth of others, can contribute to a deeper understanding of the nature of this universal yearning. My intense hope is that by moving our sometimes-obsessive attachment from an institutional version of the divine to the living experience within each of us, we can vanquish the spectre of faith-based sectarian violence that has inflicted and continues to inflict so much suffering in this world.

ONE:

GENESIS

ONE:

GENESIS

My role in the historical drama of the world began on July 23, 1941, at a time when the Luftwaffe were dropping bombs on England, Rommel's forces were battling the Allies in the deserts of Egypt, and Nazi leaders were implementing a diabolical plan to eliminate the Jewish people of Europe. It was the apocalypse of World War II, the deadliest global war in human history, lasting six years and slaughtering more than 100 million people across thirty nations. By extreme good fortune and perhaps by a stroke of fate, I was born in a bomb-free part of the theatre of war—Toronto, Canada, a country physically untouched by the destruction but whose men and women participated in the distant battlefields at a cost of many lives and injuries. I was spared the miseries endured by millions around the globe, but I never lost touch with the horror of that war. Survivor's guilt can operate over great stretches of time and geography.

I was guided into the epoch of this inferno by the skilled hands of Dr. Minerva Reid, an astonishingly accomplished woman for her time—the first female chief of surgery in North America and a member of the first Board of Directors at the Women's College Hospital in Toronto. A photograph taken of me in her arms at six months shows her dressed in a floor-length black skirt and long-sleeved cardigan, her thin white hair parted in the middle and twirled into a bun over each ear. She looks directly into the lens with a slight smile. When she attended my birth, Dr. Reid was already seventy years old, retired from her work at the hospital but still active in her private practice. For years it was a notable fact about me that I had been delivered by a woman doctor. That choice was my mother's doing.

My mother, Helen Anne Ewart, was tall, slender, and blonde. In her youth she modelled for advertisements in store catalogues, studied classical piano, and played lead parts in amateur theatricals. In a yellowing newspaper clipping from her modelling days, she looks radiant and classically beautiful, possessed of a self-confident, relaxed persona at odds with my memories of her tense personality. In September 1940, she and my father married in their twenties. In keeping with the expectations of the time, she quit work to raise me, only returning to the work force eleven years later as a salesperson at Classics Books, a prestigious Montreal book chain and later the Albert Britnell Book Shop in Toronto.

My father, Thomas Joseph Cassidy, was one of seven children of Irish Catholic stock. As the eldest child, his family anticipated he would join the priesthood. When he and my mother met in the 1930s, he was flying open-cockpit airplanes, a daring feat given the state of aviation technology at the time. He flew with my mother into the skies several times. The family story goes that she eventually clipped his wings, and he stopped flying. I think it was more likely he couldn't afford to fly and support a wife and daughter at the same time.

Raised during the Great Depression of 1929 to 1939, when banks fell into bankruptcy and millions lost their jobs, my parents were barred from attaining educational degrees, the passport to higher-paying positions. Consequently, our lifestyle was quite modest—not super poor where one occupied a cold-water flat, but a notch or two below the comfort level of a middle-class home. We rented an apartment, while our friends dwelt in houses. We never owned a car, a telling sign of a limited income. But we ate well, dressed well, and resided in a respectable neighbourhood. Despite their tight money situation, my parents always assumed I would attend university.

Dad settled into a lifelong career in the coal tar industry, specifically overseeing the setting up of processing plants. The plants he visited smelled of creosote, a distillate of tar. The odour lingered on his business suit even when he returned home. I'm always reminded of him whenever I walk past a street crew laying tar asphalt for a new road. When he retired, his company named their new tar plant after him—The Cassidy Works—marked by a plaque hanging over the entranceway. His job in the chemical industry brought me an unexpected gift. Deemed essential to the war effort, he was exempt from having to enlist to fight in Europe, which spared me the trauma of my father dying overseas at an early age.

Playing golf and snooker were two of my dad's passions, but golf was the most cherished, the one he shared with Mom. Together they spent many hours on our local nine-hole golf course, affectionately referred to as the "Rock Pile." They tried to interest me in the game, but it never took, although for a while I was fond of driving golf balls at a driving range.

My first encounter with Something-Other-Than occurred at the age of three. It is so clear in my memory. I'm seated on a sofa in the living room of our rented post-war Toronto bungalow. My mother and father must be close by, but I can't hear them or see them. I'm alone, but not lonely. From the sofa I can see the long table in the adjoining dining room. As I sit gazing at the wooden table, a ray of sunlight enters through a nearby window and lights up the centre of the table. The sight fills my chest with a sweet pain. On one hand, the sensation hurts, and on the other hand, it's as though I've come home for the first time. My three-year-old self had no knowledge of light beams representing celestial forces of love and anguish, or how these contradictions could dwell in one heart at the same moment. Why then such an intense reaction, so strong that I can vividly remember and feel it decades later?

My first encounter with the concept of a soul occurred at bedtime when my mother tucked me in and together we'd recite a popular Christian prayer for children, first published in 1784:

> Now I lay me down to sleep,
> I pray the Lord my Soul to keep.
> If I should die before I wake
> I pray the Lord my Soul to take.
>
> God bless [names of family members].

The prayer must have made an impression on me, as I've always been able to recite it without hesitation. However, it gave me little comfort. Instead, it raised in me a sense of apprehension. I didn't understand which part of me constituted my soul. If I didn't know that, how could I protect it from this scary Lord who would steal it away during the night in the event I died? And what did dying mean?

I grew up as an only child, a fact that made me an oddity in the 1940s and 1950s, when three to five children were the typical-sized family brood. I was asked several times by my friends' mothers if I was sad not to have brothers or sisters. "What will you do when your parents are no longer around?" they would say in a most solicitous manner. Their questions raised in me an odd twinge of guilt bordering on shame, as though being an only child was my fault. Later, I appreciated my status as an only child; I was spared the angst of sibling rivalry and never doubted that Mom and Dad loved me best.

Neither of my parents, despite being raised by families who attended to religious customs of prayer and church on Sundays, were firm believers. I don't ever recall hearing them discuss religion beyond a casual word or two, usually in the negative. I don't believe the concept of "God" was ever spoken of, at least in my hearing. So, it must be observed, whatever good qualities I might possess came from my parents' example and that of my extended family, not from commandments handed down from a loving or vengeful God. A child raised as a heathen can still become a civilized and peace-loving person.

Spiritual beliefs, attitudes, and practices have their genesis, as do most things, in the heart of a family backed by generations of ancestorial beliefs. My father's ancestors originated in County Cork, Ireland, arriving in Canada in the latter part of the 1800s as part of the exodus after the Irish Potato Famine. They brought with them a strong Roman Catholic faith, which they passed on to succeeding generations. They settled in southern Ontario, married, raised their children, and died there, leaving their offspring to make the final move to Toronto. The only traces of these early ancestors are found on headstones in rural church graveyards. I honour them for their courage and stamina in making the long sea journey to a country noted primarily for its snowdrifts and frozen lakes.

My paternal grandfather, Thomas Patrick Cassidy (1879–1949), worked as a tailor and in his spare time wrote poetry. A manuscript of his poems is now in my keeping. Written in the stilted syntax typical of Canadian poetry of the time, the poems contain Roman Catholic imagery and turns of phrase scattered throughout. One poem is titled "Lama Sabachthani." I had to look up what the title meant. It originated in the opening words of Psalm 22: "Eli Eli Lama Sabachthani," which translates as "My God, my God, why hast Thou forsaken me?" These are the words the Bible tells us Jesus shouted as he hung on the cross, feeling abandoned by God, his father, and with the sins of the world weighing on his soul.

Lama Sabachthani

Friend, I too have sought Thee sorrowing,
Yet never found Thee in one vaunted place:
Stones have I broken, nor heard one fluttering wing,
Wood opened, nor found of Thee one trace.

Within, where Thou hast said Thy kingdom is,
I looked once keenly, saw the broken thrones;
All else was dark as in the land of Dis—
And full of rottenness and dead men's bones.

Yet once a Hill was given to my sight,—
Round like a skull, thereon a Hideous Tree
And I heard ring across the startled night,—
"Why Oh! my God, hast Thou forsaken me."[1]

Several other of his poems contained references to "Olivet," the Mount of Olives in Jerusalem described in the Bible as the place from which Jesus ascended to heaven. At the foot of Mount Olive is the Garden of Gethsemane, where, it is said, Jesus accepted that the time had come for him to be betrayed, arrested, and crucified the next day. My grandfather referred to Olivet in this verse:

---

1. Thomas Patrick Cassidy, circa 1925.

Forgive these feet that eager pace
Where pathway and world's highway met.
But hesitating, turn and trace
Backward sad steps from Olivet.

My grandfather Cassidy died when I was seven. I have no recollection of ever meeting him. I often wonder what thoughts and religious encounters drove him to write these poems. My mother said her father-in-law was not an affectionate man, leaving the emotional nurturing of his children to his wife. Today, I marvel at what drove my grandfather, after a day spent cutting and sewing suits, to return in the evening to his wife and seven children, eat dinner, and then climb the stairs to his study to write religious poetry. What testimony to the power of the yearning for a religious faith in a person's life.

My father never spoke of his father to me. It's not difficult to understand the roots of their estrangement. In the eyes of my grandfather, Dad committed the most unforgivable of sins—he left the true Catholic faith. As the eldest son in a Catholic family, it was anticipated my father would enter the priesthood and become his family's offering to the Church. For a time in his youth, he had served as an altar boy, but that wasn't enough to anchor his faith. My mother told me that when Dad spoke to his father of his decision to leave the Catholic Church, the response was swift and cutting: "This will kill your mother." My grandmother Cassidy died five years later, although probably not due to my father's religious defection.

My mother's ancestors, the Ewarts, arrived in Canada from Northumberland, England, around 1800 and settled into small towns northwest of Toronto. Their offspring married Irish immigrants whose ancestors came from Antrim County, Ireland, and Yorkshire, England, creating a third generation of Canadians of Irish and English heritage. Once in Canada, they aligned themselves with the Protestant denomination known as the United Church of Canada. A part of my ancestry comes from Holland. My maternal grandmother's maiden name was Ouderkirk, a Dutch word meaning a dwelling near an old church. I know nothing about this part of my family tree, but I expect these Dutch immigrants favoured the teachings of the Dutch Reformed Church, a major branch of Protestantism that emphasized the sovereignty of God and the authority of the Bible.

My maternal grandfather, Archibald McCallum Ewart ("Archie"), also died early in my life, and like my grandfather Cassidy, I don't recall meeting him. However, Grandpa Archie left behind a detailed journal of his work in the Ontario northland, which makes me feel I knew him. He was a skilled musician able to play many instruments, with the fiddle being his preferred one. He headed up his own dance band known as "Archibald Ewart and His Harmony Orchestra." The band played on the radio in the 1940s and in iconic venues like the Palace Pier dance hall, popular in Toronto at that time.

His day job was as an electrician. For many years he worked in Val d'Or, Quebec, at the Shawkey Gold Mining Company installing electrical wiring in the mining shafts. His diary for the years 1934–1936 recounted in vivid detail how he almost drowned when the pit crew accidentally let water flow into the mine shaft while he was still at the bottom of the shaft with his crew. He also left a fifteen-page account of the hard lives experienced by the multi-ethnic and Indigenous peoples in Canada's northland. He would go to cafés with his fiddle and join in spontaneous music sessions that included Cuban, French, and mulatto musicians playing Irish folk tunes. He wrote about almost freezing to death crossing a frozen lake in snow up to his armpits. The next morning the frozen body of another miner was found on the same lake trail Archie had travelled the previous night.

I have no idea what spiritual life Archie enjoyed. He was a dynamic personality who had the responsibility of two younger sisters thrust on him when he was only fourteen. My mother and her sisters adored him. I wish I had known him.

Although God was not spoken of in my home, I eventually became aware of a religious tension simmering below the surface, which could break through at the most trivial trigger. As a child, I had no understanding of what it meant for my Protestant mother and my Catholic father to marry, to have what was then rather quaintly referred to as a "mixed marriage." Even though Dad had left the Catholic faith several years before he married my mother, she suspected his siblings blamed her for their brother's loss of faith. Her failing to convert to Catholicism made it even less likely he would return to the True Faith. In childhood, I rarely saw my Cassidy aunts, uncles, and cousins.

My mother and father had an affectionate, stable marriage, rarely arguing. There was no shouting or throwing of objects or emotional terrorism. If a disagreement did bubble up, the vocal hostilities were kept outside my hearing. Dad was a quiet and kindly man, an introvert who didn't relish debate or open confrontation. Mom was much more the extrovert, up for a verbal spar if any personal slight was detected in a conversational exchange.

The religious divide sometimes took the form of bitter words from my mother, who keenly felt the unspoken rejection of her husband's family. Once at dinner she mentioned that she had ordered school photographs of me to send to her sisters and brother. "I would have ordered copies for your brothers and sisters," she added, "if they were at all interested." My dad pushed the food around his plate and said nothing.

On the few occasions my father's siblings visited our home, the undercurrent of estrangement was covered up with polite conversation. However, one Friday evening the religious divide poked its way into the centre of attention. My father's sister and her husband came for dinner. My mother was nervous about the visit. At the last moment, she remembered the Roman Catholic custom of abstaining from meat on Friday, fish being the only acceptable substitute. She had no fish in the house and had already prepared a meat dish. I was fifteen at the time, and in my adolescent ignorance I scoffed at such a silly rule. "What difference does it make?" I told my mother. "Meat or fish, they're the same. They won't mind." But it did make a difference. My father's sister and her husband sat stony-faced at the dining table while we waited for eight o'clock to roll around, at which point, apparently, the meat fast could be broken. The thick silence around the dinner table seemed to last forever. My father said nothing to lighten the atmosphere, and neither did my uncle, who had converted to Catholicism when he married into the Cassidy clan. As a convert, my uncle had learned to let his wife take the lead in Roman Catholic observances.

A few times Dad gently mocked religion. Once, sitting at the kitchen table while filling in the Canadian census form, he hesitated a moment, his pen poised over the *Religious Affiliation* box. "Helen, I know what I'm going to write in this box," he said. "I'm going to enter *Shintoism* as my religious affiliation."

"Shintoism? What's that?" she asked.

"Some weird Japanese religion no one has heard of. It'll drive the census bureaucrats crazy."

He chuckled as he filled in the form. My mother joined in the laughter.

Despite my mother's disregard of religious practices, at the age of four she sent me to a Protestant Sunday school. As she told the story, I came home after the first class, frustrated by the "silly stories" they told. Mom was amused by what I reported, almost satisfied, as though my reaction confirmed her opinion of traditional religion. Whenever she retold this story to others, it was delivered as a gentle mocking of all religion, but Catholicism in particular. I continued to attend Sunday school at the United Church of Canada and occasionally participated in church services into my early teens. I don't recall my parents ever attending with me. Why, I've always wondered, did they bother to send me to church? Was it a way to be a part of a respectable community, or a way to expose me to religion just in case the devil was real, and I'd need an ally against him? I never found out why.

On another occasion, when I was twelve, the director of the Sunday school at our local United Church asked me to teach the younger children the parables of Jesus. I was surprised at being asked, since my understanding of the parables was very thin. But in my heart of hearts, I was proud to have been chosen. When I told my father about my new responsibility, he laughed. "That's definitely a case of the blind leading the blind." I quit my teaching post the next Sunday.

The Christmas season would bring out a round of sabre rattling from my mother when my father's family would send holiday cards featuring ornate illustrations of the Virgin Mary and Baby Jesus in the manger, surrounded by three bearded kings. Mom saw the Christian iconography on the cards as a dig at my father's lapsed Catholic faith. The Cassidy clan may not have meant anything by their choice of cards, but past religious frictions had already sown seeds of distrust in my mother.

On my mother's side of the family, the friction between Roman Catholicism and Protestantism erupted at the birth of her sister's daughter. My aunt, like my mother, had married into a Catholic family. While my uncle wasn't a practising Catholic, his family kept after him about the spiritual danger his daughter was in. If she wasn't baptized in the Catholic Church, my cousin was doomed to hell and damnation for eternity. Even though my aunt and uncle had agreed to raise their daughter as a Protestant, at the urgings of his family he had her secretly baptized as a Catholic. It appears that was the breaking point in my aunt and uncle's marriage. They separated soon after, and my uncle sought custody of his daughter, all the way to the Supreme Court of Canada. In the end, my aunt retained custody.

With the passage of time, the religious divide in Canada between the Roman Catholic Church and the various Protestant denominations became less strident. When my husband (a lapsed Anglican) and I (a confused agnostic) were married twenty years later by a Unitarian minister, there was no visible fuss in Dad's family. His siblings were warm and welcoming to me and my new husband.

———

Religious divides not only surfaced in my home but also in my school life. None of my high school friends spoke of their religious views, if indeed they had any. Religion just didn't exist as a relevant topic in our busy social lives. Brenda was my closest friend throughout senior high school and university. We hung out together at all the usual soda fountains, dances, and parties, and at university we joined the same sorority. After our initiation, we discovered that the sorority regularly held a solemn ceremony, where candles were lit and passed around the circle to the accompaniment of quotes from Christian scripture. I was surprised by this religious turn in a group I had joined for the crass purpose of partying and meeting boys. The unexpected ritual gave me the giggles, as it did Brenda. Despite my mocking reaction, one biblical quote in the ceremony impressed me. It came from the thirteenth chapter of St. Paul's First Epistle to the Corinthians: "For now we see in a mirror, darkly, but then face to face. Now I know in part, but then shall I know just as I also am known. And now abide faith, hope, love, these three; but the greatest of these is love." I didn't really understand these arcane words, but their essence shone through and still touches me to this day.

Amongst our sorority sisters was a girl named Moira, who took religious matters much more seriously than Brenda and I. Moira was Presbyterian and a regular churchgoer. Amongst ourselves, Brenda and I often mocked Moira's religiosity. That all changed when Brenda met her future husband, a seminary student studying to be a Presbyterian minister. Knowing Brenda's cavalier attitude to religion, I was surprised she decided to marry into the clergy of a religion, but I said nothing. As her best friend, I expected to be asked to serve as her maid of honour. Instead, she chose Moira, a faithful, practising Presbyterian. Her betrayal was like a spear to the heart. Brenda had passed over our long friendship to curry favour with her Presbyterian fiancé. I couldn't bear to speak with her, which was hard to do, as we attended the same classes every day. Finally, she cornered me and asked me what was wrong. When I told her, she invited me to be a bridesmaid. I refused. The bond of our friendship had been broken over a religious preference and it never recovered, even though I visited her ten years later at her husband's vicarage in Manitoba and thirty years later at a sorority reunion. By then her marriage to the minister was over and she had remarried. Her ex-husband had died from a bee sting during a religious conference in Florida.

Despite spending my adolescent years in Montreal, where the Catholic Church was supreme both politically and spiritually, I only recall encountering one symbol of this intense faith—Saint Joseph's Oratory in Montreal. It's Canada's largest church and possesses the third-largest dome in the world. One day at fifteen I visited Saint Joseph's with my parents. The oratory was built by Brother André in honour of Jesus' worldly father, Joseph, who was said to be a carpenter. It stands on the summit of Mount Royal in the middle of the island of Montreal. Pilgrims approach the shrine by an imposing flight of ninety-nine steps. The more devout and able-bodied can choose to climb the stairs on their knees to show humility and as a penance for their sins.

The massive interior of the oratory was overwhelming and, to my way of thinking, gloomy and threatening. Ten Protestant churches wouldn't fill up the space taken by this one basilica. The high dome was complemented by thousands of votive candles, stained glass windows, and multi-angled arches. The most dramatic sight of all was the thousands of crutches left hanging on the walls by pilgrims who had visited during the lifetime of Brother André, the oratory's founding saint.

Despite being midday, the level of lighting inside the basilica was dim, caused in part by the dark wood of the rows and rows of pews and what seemed an excessive use of candles for lighting. I entered one of the pew rows and stumbled on a piece of wood lying on the floor.

"Who left this wood here?" I asked my mother, indignant at being thrown off balance.

"It's not wood," she replied. "It's a prayer bench put there so you can kneel as you pray."

Ridiculous! was my thought at the time. What is praying anyway? Why do people need to kneel to pray? And what is that scent in the air, that sort of earthy, musky smell? "Incense," my mother said, "it's incense." Many years later, in a totally different context, I came to love the scent.

Overall, St. Joseph's gave off a creepy vibration. Even at fifteen, I sensed the basilica was a showplace built to intimidate worshippers. The immensity of the building didn't encourage an intimate relationship with God. I was in awe of the space around me, but it was an awe based in fear, a fear of being swallowed up. Later, I read that the bodily heart of Brother André, the shrine's founding saint, was preserved in a glass jar in the basement, on view for the public. I can't recall if we saw the heart that day. Probably not, or I would have remembered.

TWO:

THE WAY OF
THE BOOK

TWO:

THE WAY OF THE BOOK

B ooks have served as my mentors from an early age. My mother introduced me to the world of books when I was eight years old. I clearly remember the day she took me to a downtown branch of the Toronto Public Library. I had never seen books in such abundance—shelves and shelves bursting with printed words, photographs, and paintings of worldly splendours, from walruses to salamanders, Egyptian pyramids to Chinese rickshaws, and towering waterfalls to forest streams. Despite my reputation in the family as a talkative little girl, in this instance I found myself at a loss for words. I walked away from the library, one hand holding my mother's coat, the other gripping three slim volumes. I was so eager to get home and start reading. I wasn't sure exactly what I had seen in the building my mother called a "library." Whatever its name, in my child's mind I knew it was an important place. Years later, I had a similar feeling when I first entered the main Reading Room of the British Museum, keenly aware that every book published in the English language could be found in the stacks. Standing under the museum's spectacular two-acre glass roof, I had the sensation of having entered the cerebral cortex of a giant brain.

From that day at the Toronto Public Library onwards, books became my touchstone for solving whatever puzzle perplexed me. Whenever I couldn't see my way through a complexity in my life, I would head for a bookstore or a library and invariably discover the book I needed to give me perspective on my problem. I wasn't a disciplined reader who methodically chewed my way through prescribed lists of literary classics. My approach was much more serendipitous. Standing amongst shelves of books in a university library or in a bookstore, a subtle force field from a particular title would beckon me. I'd scan the spine, pull the title off the shelf, flip it open to the title page, and then move on to the first chapter. If the book was what I needed, the words and phrases immediately leapt off the page and made neural connections to my unconscious. "This is it, this will do just fine," I'd mutter to myself. Once inside a book and engrossed in its content, an immense network of footnotes and bibliographies linked me to related titles. Travelling these bibliographic trails through a jungle of knowledge, then suddenly coming upon a jewel of deep understanding, was for me the most exciting of mental activities.

It was, therefore, natural for me to turn to books as my primary resource for searching for that Something-Other-Than. Certainly, I would have preferred to experience the divine directly through an inner vision or hearing words spoken from a burning bush. Unfortunately, I had no idea how to make that happen. Christian theology, I read, was adamant that God would decide when and where to reveal his presence to me. It all came down to a mysterious something called God's grace, defined as an undeserved love and favour given out by God, which has nothing to do with anything one has done or not done. It appeared, until I was struck by this holy bolt of revelation, I would have to make do with second-hand accounts found in sacred texts and religious confessions. Not exactly the original experience I was seeking, but at least a place to begin.

As it turned out, pursuing the divine through the written word was a very appropriate way to begin my quest. In the New Testament of the Bible, John 1:1 opens with the sentence "In the beginning was the Word, and the Word was with God, and the Word was God." Christians view Jesus Christ as God's word made flesh. For Muslims, the words of their sacred text the Qur'an are believed to be the direct words of God as spoken through the Prophet Muhammad. In the Hindu sacred text, the Rig Veda, the rishis, or wise men who compiled the spiritual truths over the centuries, considered the "word" as a metaphor for the transcendent impersonal force that held the cosmos together. In one Vedic hymn, it is declared:

> First there is Brahman, Lord of all,
> With whom is vach, the Word,
> And the Word, verily, is Brahman.

The psychologist C. G. Jung best expressed what I hoped to attain by reading my way to God. In a BBC TV interview held toward the end of his life, when asked if he believed in the existence of God, Jung replied, "I don't believe there is a God; I know there is a God." In my reading I wasn't looking for a belief system, or even a faith, but an inner knowing of the truth. Jung had followed the path of psychology to reach his inner truth. I needed to find my path, and initially that way would be through the accounts left by other seekers—the way of the book.

Plunging into the voluminous world literature of religion and soul work can be overwhelming. Contradictory beliefs and lack of rigorous definition of concepts can leave one feeling muddled. How does one determine who speaks the holy truth? How does one hold on to the quest in the face of this lack of certainty? What is the best attitude to take while advancing through the flood of revelations? By chance one day I came upon a quote attributed to the Greek philosopher Plato: "How will you go about finding that thing the nature of which is totally unknown to you?" This quote described my conundrum perfectly. I was on a quest to uncover the source of my yearning for an invisible, mysterious something, but I had no idea where to look for this rarest of entities or how I'd recognize it when I happened upon it.

A few days of research drew forth one answer, most famously articulated in 1817 by the Romantic poet John Keats in a letter to his brother George Keats. It was necessary, he proclaimed with great conviction, for a man of achievement, especially in literature, to possess a state of being he called *negative capability*, by which he meant for the person to be "capable of being in uncertainties, Mysteries, doubts, without any irritable reaching after fact and reason ... [being] content with half knowledge." Keats trusted the truth of the imagination and the heart's affections above reason and knowledge.[2]

Maintaining such a relaxed attitude towards uncertainty would be a daunting challenge for me, as I strive for stability and predictability in my intellectual landscape. I want to be certain I've nailed the truth of a matter. Obviously in my search for an answer to the Great Mystery, I was going to have to change my attitude and learn to live in a world of shifting perceptions that wouldn't sit still for me. Logic and reason wouldn't be the only

---

2.   Duncan Wu, ed., *Romanticism: An Anthology*, 3rd ed. (Oxford: Blackwell, 2006), 1351.

way to reach my goal; it would also require a large portion of imagination and heart.

The first author to give me a wide perspective on religious thinking was Jiddu Krishnamurti, a modern Indian philosopher. In his book, *Freedom from the Known*, he rejected the mantle of guru and messiah laid on him by the Theosophical Society, a popular cult that preached a blend of Buddhism and Indian Brahmanism. Instead, Krishnamurti claimed to be simply a teacher sharing ideas with those who cared to listen. I found his lectures easy to read, and he spoke his ideas in a blunt, straightforward manner. His focus wasn't on seeking an external divinity for the answers to life's problems, but for each person to become more self-aware. Facing our own life was what mattered. His most quoted saying was "Truth is a pathless land, and you cannot approach it by any path whatsoever, by any religion, by any sect." He didn't believe in an external deity called God who had all the answers and gave all the commandments. Humans invented God, he claimed, so we would feel more safe, secure, and loved. When worshipping God, we're merely worshipping an image of ourselves. All the religious rituals and textual dictums are a waste of time, so much silliness and entertainment to cover over the dark sides of our psyche, our brutality, violence, greed, ambition, and endless sorrow. Not finding "this nameless thing of a thousand names," his phrase for my Something-Other-Than, we look to someone else to tell us what is right or wrong, rather than finding the answers in ourselves.[3] In the process we become second-hand people and cultivate a faith in an external saviour or an ideal to which we cling, standing ready to commit any level of violence to preserve that faith's perspective. We must foremost

---

3. Jiddu Krishnamurti, *Freedom from the Known* (London: Gollancz, 1972), 9.

understand ourselves; nobody else on Earth or in heaven can save us from ourselves.

Reading Krishnamurti's lectures was a bracing experience, somewhat like having a glass of cold water splashed in your face. While he can rid you of many illogical thoughts and behaviours—a good thing—he leaves you up the proverbial creek without the essential paddle. He tears down the time-tested comforts of faith and pleasant distractions, only to leave his audience with the terrifying admonition to know one's own self. His writings do not provide the specifics for such an under-taking, reputed to require guidelines and plentiful support or risk the possibility of a mental breakdown. Still, I support his attitude of being skeptical about second-hand knowledge; he insists we must rely on direct experience, a view that resonated with me at the time and does to this day.

I found another outstanding account of the major themes in a spiritual search in William James's book, *The Varieties of Religious Experience: A Study in Human Nature.* James was a renowned American philosopher and psychologist, brother of the famous novelist Henry James. Published as a collection of university lectures in 1902, the book caused much excitement at the time of its publication and eventually ranked as one of the most influential books of the twentieth century. It remains in print to this day.

While William James was critical of many aspects of orga-nized religions, he was also sympathetic to the fact that striving for a spiritual perspective on the world had been a major thread running through the evolution of humankind since the begin-nings of recorded time. This need for a cosmic explanation of the beautiful yet terrifying reality in which humans find them-selves was, in his view, an essential function of human nature that held great value for individuals and the collective society. He characterized the basis of religion as the belief "... that there is an unseen order, and that our supreme good lies in harmoniously adjusting ourselves thereto."[4]

James's thinking was unique in that he took into account both the tenets of organized religions and the experience of the individual. It must be remembered, he declared, that the individual experience rather than the religious trappings of ritual and prayer remains the keystone of true religion. The body of doctrines, dogmas, and rituals conducted inside the precincts of churches, synagogues, and mosques is a derivative, second-hand expression of the original spark of divinity revealed at a point in time to one person. In exceptional circumstances, such as those of Moses, the Christ, and Prophet Muhammad, the accounts were written up, annotated, and converted into sacred scriptures. In turn, these scriptures became the basis for grand theologies and rituals designed to guide others who had not undergone these experiences. Why the spiritual encounters of only a few persons in human history generated such a universal response is hard to explain. Perhaps it was simply these select few had greater powers of persuasion and verbal expression than the others. Or, traditional believers might say, these great ones truly connected with God; the lesser visionaries were false prophets. This belief that the divine truth is revealed to only a select few means that most of humanity follows the rules and rituals of a handful of designated prophets. Over time, their theologies became carved in spiritual stone and the stage was set for holy wars and religious persecutions against those who stepped outside prescribed parameters of faith and theology.

Books have long played a critical role as purveyors of the word of God. The followers of Islam, Judaism, and Christianity call themselves "People of the Book" to highlight their reliance

---

4. William James, *The Varieties of Religious Experience* (New York: The Modern Library, 2002), 61.

on the written word of God. Eventually, such books became sacred objects in themselves, spawning a set of complex rules around their handling. For instance, it's not permissible for the Judaic Torah to lie on the ground. If, accidentally, the text is dropped on the floor, it must be picked up and given a kiss. In courts of law, it was and still is customary for witnesses to swear on a copy of the Bible as a security that what they are about to say is the truth. The Islamic Qur'an is not to be left open after reading. Even today, to desecrate the Qur'an runs the risk of incurring banishment, beatings, or even death.

Through my attendance at Sunday school, I grew up with a passing familiarity with the Christian Bible. But my knowledge was definitely on the thin side. In my childhood home we didn't possess a copy of the Bible until I had to buy one for my high school English class. However, growing up in a Christian culture and society, I was familiar with the basic tenets of Christianity as described in the Bible. But I was totally ignorant of other sacred scriptures, such as the Jewish Torah, the Qur'an of Islam, and Hinduism's Bhagavad Gita and the Upanishads. I never delved into the Torah or the Qur'an, but I did read a good part of the sacred texts of Hinduism, especially the Bhagavad Gita. Of all the scared literature I've read, the Hindu commentaries strike me as the closest to the truth, deep yet flexible enough to be capable of incorporating enhancements without damaging the basic premises.

Unlike Christianity and Islam, the Hindu religion doesn't feature a single holy figure who speaks the word of God. Instead, Hinduism spreads the words of God through an intricate body of sacred texts. Initially, the word "Hinduism" didn't refer to a religion but was a word adopted by the British colonial power of the nineteenth century to refer to the Indian worship of several gods like Parvati, Brahma, Lord Krishna, and Vishnu. The worship of these gods lacked a common theological core. Instead, the core of the Hindu religion was experienced through reading and preparing commentaries on their sacred texts.

The most ancient of these texts is the Vedas (1700–1100 BCE), followed by the Upanishads (800–500 BC), and the Bhagavad Gita. The Vedic texts, it is said, were received by scholars directly from God and passed on to succeeding generations by word of mouth and later compiled into Sanskrit by Hindu sages and saints known as rishis. Modern commentaries on the Vedas simply assert that God is the source of all knowledge, and that his truth is contained in the Vedic scriptures that everyone is required to study. While I was never able to absorb the pantheon of Hindu gods and the aspects of the human soul they personified, I found these sacred texts provided masterful portrayals of states of consciousness.

The Upanishads depict the universe as a multifaceted yet interconnected cosmos with a single, unifying principle behind its apparent diversity. This principle is called brahman, the one true ultimate God that cannot be seen or touched but is eternal and everlasting. It constitutes the unchanging, permanent, and highest reality. The brahman resides in the core of the individual, where it's known as the atman, the Eastern version of the Christian soul. The Upanishads are highly revered and considered a great source of spiritual wisdom. They celebrate a state of consciousness that lies beyond thought, a transcendental realm beyond words. The emphasis is on the direct attainment of spiritual enlightenment (the Absolute) rather than depending on intellectual concepts. Through meditation and the guidance of an enlightened teacher or guru, a person can realize for himself/herself an experience of the Infinite. The love expressed in Christianity through the worship of Jesus and in Islam through the worship of Allah is reserved in Hinduism for the teacher or guru who guides the seeker in comprehending the sacred texts.

There are many magnificent and insightful passages in the Upanishads. Here is one quote taken from the Katha Upanishad that describes the pure universal Self or atman:

> The Self lies hidden,
> And is not openly displayed.
> But It is known to those of subtle insight,
>   whose vision is purified and clear.
>
> The wise man's senses are governed by his mind.
> His mind is governed by his intellect.
> His intellect is governed by his active self.
> And his active self is governed by the silent Self.
>
> Wake up!
> Seek the Truth!
> Rise above ignorance!
> Search out the best teachers,
>   And through them find the Truth.
> But beware!
>   "The path is narrow," the sages warn,
>   "sharp as a razor's edge,
>   most difficult to tread."[5]

The Upanishads are amazing in how they define ideas or concepts that are, in essence, boundless and invisible to the senses. In the following two passages from the Mundaka Upanishad, the sacred text describes the attributes of the Self in relation to the Eternal, without making mention of a particular divinity:

> The Self is all-knowing,

---

5. Alistair Shearer and Peter Russell, trans., *The Upanishads* (London: Unwin Paperbacks, 1989), 73.

it is all-understanding,
and to it belongs all glory.
It is pure consciousness,
dwelling in the heart of all
in the divine citadel of Brahma,
There is no space it does not fill.[6]

[The eternal is]
that which cannot be seen and is beyond
thought,
which is without cause or parts,
which neither perceives nor acts,
which is unchanging, all-pervading,
omni-present subtler than the subtlest,
That is the Eternal which the wise know to be
the source of all.[7]

After the Vedas and the Upanishads, a third sacred Hindu text, the Bhagavad Gita (Song of the Lord), is considered the most influential scripture to come down through the ages in India. I read the Gita extensively and was deeply affected by its words. Written as a dialogue between Krishna, the avatar of the Hindu god Vishnu, and Arjuna, a young warrior prince, the Gita on the surface delves into the pros and cons of warfare. However, the real subject doesn't concern a historical battle but the war that rages inside each of us in our struggle for self-realization. In the end, the Gita evolves into a spiritual lesson on how through selfless devotion to Krishna, the ordinary person can transcend greed, selfishness, and partiality in the prosaic duties of daily life through an awareness of the Supreme Reality.

---

6. Shearer and Russell, trans., *The Upanishads*, 35.
7. Shearer and Russell, trans., *The Upanishads*, 24.

Many versions of the Gita have been published with different translators. My heavily underlined copy of the Gita stands out on my bookcase by virtue of its bright orange cover with the title *The Holy Geeta: Commentary by Swami Chinmayananda* in gold lettering across the front cover. The book is thick, but the pages are tissue-paper thin, gradually turning yellow with age and heavy use. The contents of the Gita brought about my most profound acquaintance with the potential nature of Something-Other-Than.

The astonishing instance started on a Monday morning as I travelled to downtown Toronto on a commuter train. I had spent the weekend at a yoga retreat, where I'd been introduced to the words in the Bhagavad Gita. I'd eagerly bought a copy at the retreat's bookstore but hadn't yet found time to delve into it. I settled into the commuter run, grateful that I had managed to claim a seat during the morning rush hour. I took the Gita out of my briefcase and opened it at random. In seconds, the words pulled me into the heart of the text. The voices of the passengers and the rumbling of the wheels on the train tracks faded away into utter silence. In the stillness, each word of the Gita dropped into my mind like a pebble thrown into a pond, carving a space for each word to echo and linger in my mind forever.

I continued in this enhanced state of consciousness for the entire trip. As the train pulled into Union Station, the voices of my fellow passengers registered again, although still at a low level. I slowly stood up from my seat and joined the crush of passengers exiting out of the sliding doors. Walking along the crowded platform and down a flight of stairs to the concourse, I descended even further underground into the bowels of the subway. Throughout this time, I walked as in a dream, each step propelled forward by an inner force unconnected to my conscious mind. I was reminded of romantic movies where lovers run across a field of grasses and flowers in slow motion, each step suspended in mid-air. All this time, hardly a sound reached my ears, yet I was acutely aware of the crowds about me and knew where I was headed.

This strange state of consciousness lasted another hour, even while I worked in my office. Gradually, the muffled sensation of the material world lifted and assumed its normal dominance. Days later, I tried to capture the effect of this experience in a poem:

The Moment

I'm cradled in the arms of time,
No longer stressed and strained
By being here or there
By yesterday, day here, or day to come.

Airy puffs of silence fill my ears,
Muffling the echoes of a cacophonous world
Where strange creatures mouth stillborn words
And glide in a reverie of slow beatitude.

I see your marks upon the page,
Here a word, a comma, space, and phrase,
Yet never do I see you, rather feel you
Move in the blood and marrow of me now.

Whose words are these, whose letters
Pierce the skull's all-seeing sense
With visual parades of combinations new and fresh,
Just born into me, this world of singularity?

The words flow through my bones
Striking shuddering blows at me, them
And us, leaving a yearning, a reaching for it all,
Almost there, yet still beyond the finger's tip.

This strange encounter drew me to read accounts of other people's experience of the divine, that Something-Other-Than. I sought out the circumstances of the first spark of divinity that seeded the three major faiths—Christianity, Islam, and Hinduism—and inspired billions of people around the globe to follow their example in awakening the spirit within. The divine encounter between human and God, between the individual and the mysterious sacred, is frequently described in terms both terrifying and joyful, overpowering and peaceful. A full-blast encounter with the divine is said to sometimes transform people in unfavourable ways. Unable to absorb what has happened, an individual may fall to pieces psychologically and be unable to function in the secular world. It's thought that the transcendent light from these events needs to be moderated through priestly rites and the sacred texts of a well-structured religion. C. G. Jung is quoted as saying that the function of religion is to protect us from the experience of God.

The most dramatic and detailed account of a meeting between the divine and a human being is that of the Prophet Muhammad's encounter with Allah's divine presence. According to the sacred Qur'an, in 610 CE, Muhammad communicated with God in a cave on Mount Hira' near Mecca during the religious Arabic holiday of Ramadan. He was forty years old, a respected merchant in the city of Mecca, and a family man with several children. He was religious and often meditated and distributed alms to the poor from his cave retreat on Mount Hira'. He was familiar with the stories of the previous prophets Noah, Lot, Abraham, Moses, and Jesus, and with their foretelling of a great messiah who would arrive one day. According to contemporary accounts, Muhammad had no intention or wish to be that messiah.

While sleeping in his cave, Muhammad felt himself gripped in an overpowering embrace by a devastating, terrifying presence that squeezed the breath from his body. A voice commanded him to recite the words before him. While he could not read or write, the words came pouring unbidden from Muhammad's lips. These words became the first instalment of the great Islamic sacred text known as the holy Qur'an.

Initially, this vision filled Muhammad with despair. He didn't understand what was happening and later found it almost impossible to describe the encounter. He fled the cave and started to climb to the summit of Mount Hira', where he intended to fling himself off the mountain to his death. Instead, he was blocked by the sight of a mighty being that filled the horizons all about him. This being he later referred to as Gabriel, the spirit of revelation and a transcendent presence well beyond the usual categories of space and human traits.

Muhammad turned away from Gabriel's presence and ran down the slope of Mount Hira' in anguish, falling on his knees before his wife, who wrapped him in a cloak and held him until his fear abated. For the next twenty-three years, Allah's messages continued to be revealed to Muhammad, who spread the words amongst his people. He faced much resistance in getting his tribe to accept Allah's message, but eventually Islam became the second most practised religion in the world, spreading to an estimated 1.8 billion followers worldwide. After his death, Muhammad's words were compiled under the instruction of his successor, Abu Bakr, and turned into what became known as the sacred text of the Qur'an. Today, the Muslim declaration of faith reads, "I bear witness that there is no God but Allah and that Muhammad is his messenger."

Unlike the narrative surrounding Muhammad's life, we don't find an account in the Bible of the moment when Jesus first experienced the divine. In their doctrine, Christians believe

Jesus was fully human and fully divine from the beginning of time. Being both God and human, Jesus remains one person, the son of God, incarnated or "made flesh" by being conceived in the womb of a woman. Jesus didn't need to go out into the world to find God. According to the Christian creed, Jesus Christ was always a part of God, a human form through which God chose to work his way in the world.

From my reading, I learned that encounters with the divine come to people in various forms and under widely varying circumstances. From these scattered accounts, it's difficult to extrapolate an all-encompassing theory about what the universe of Something-Other-Than might look like. We need more examples to define the commonalities. I consider that the glimpses of the divine documented to this point represent only the tip of a mighty spiritual mountain range invisible to the human senses. I've begun to collect spiritual accounts that give a varied representation of these rare moments when the invisible infinite breaks through the veil of the material world.

In *The Varieties of Religious Experience*, William James recounts a divine revelation experienced by a clergyman of the nineteenth century:

> I remember the night, and almost the very spot on
> the hilltop, where my soul opened out, as it were,
> into the Infinite, and there was a rushing together
> of the two worlds, the inner and the outer. It was
> deep calling onto deep—the deep that my own
> struggle had opened up within being answered by
> the unfathomable deep without, reaching beyond
> the stars. I stood alone with Him who had made
> me, and all the beauty of the world, and love, and
> sorrow, and even temptation. I did not seek Him,
> but felt the perfect unison of my spirit with His.

The ordinary sense of things around me faded. For the moment nothing but an ineffable joy and exultation remained.... Having once felt the presence of God's spirit, I have never lost it again for long.[8]

James also gives an account of a cosmic state of consciousness experienced by a Canadian psychiatrist, Dr. Bucke, at the beginning of the twentieth century. This account struggles with the limits of the intellect in explaining such an event.

All at once, without warning of any kind, I found myself wrapped in a flame-coloured cloud. For an instant, I thought of fire, an immense conflagration somewhere close by in that great city; the next, I knew that the fire was within myself. Directly afterward there came upon me a sense of exultation, of immense joyousness accompanied by or immediately followed by intellectual illumination impossible to describe. Among other things, I did not merely come to believe, but, I saw that the universe is not composed of dead matter, but is, on the contrary, a living Presence; I became conscious in myself of eternal life.... I saw that all men are immortal; ... that the foundation principle of the world, of all the worlds, is what we call love, and that the happiness of each and all is in the long run absolutely certain.[9]

Christian mystics frequently describe intense states of consciousness experienced when their spirit is exalted to a

---

8. James, *The Varieties of Religious Experience*, 76.
9. James, *The Varieties of Religious Experience*, 435.

knowledge of things divine. These encounters with God or Jesus are called raptures. I found a quote from such an event drawn from the writings of the Catholic saint St. Thérèse of Lisieux (1873–1897), more popularly known as the Little Flower of Jesus, or simply, the Little Flower:

> A few days after the oblation of myself to God's Merciful Love, I was in the choir, beginning the Way of the Cross, when I felt myself suddenly wounded by a dart of fire so ardent that I thought I should die. I do not know how to explain this transport; there is no comparison to describe the intensity of that flame. It seemed as though an invisible force plunged me wholly into fire … But oh! What fire! What sweetness![10]

In his essays, James characterized these states of mystical consciousness in three ways: they defy expression to others; their insight into depths of truth are ones unavailable to the intellect; the mystic feels as though his will is in abeyance, and he is being grasped and held by a superior power.

Recently, I read an account of a young man of thirty, at a loss for a direction in his life, who in 1974 was driving alone along a coastal road in New Zealand Woods. Between one lamppost and the next, the man suddenly became aware of being taken over by an immense, overwhelming power outside his car, a power he took to be a spiritual call from God, one he couldn't refuse. He didn't see a light or any other object or person. All he remembered was the car rising as he sat in the driver's seat. After the car descended, he pulled over to the side of the road, got out, and fell to his knees in awe and prayer. The next day he

---

10. St. Thérèse of Lisieux https://ecatholic2000.com/therese/sos15.shtml.

arranged to return to England and prepare for ordination in the Church of England.

This written account cries out for more confirming detail, but this insufficiency is typical of divine encounters where words cannot convey the momentous nature of what has happened. The effect of this event on the young man's life was transformational. After taking Holy Orders in the Church of England, he served for over thirty years in a poor parish in Northern England, refusing all offers of advancement in the church hierarchy. His recent biography, written by his son after his death, included an introduction by the Archbishop of Canterbury. His daughter also entered the church, where she now leads her own parish.

A long-time friend, knowing I was writing this memoir, recounted to me her glimpse of the invisible world, providing rare details of the dramatic aftereffect of her encounter with the divine:

> My experience with what I came to think of as a spiritual awakening happened twenty-five years ago in a restaurant. At the time, I had no spiritual life, no belief in God.
>
> That wasn't always the case. As a child, I attended Sunday school, where my mother taught at the United Church. My dad was a firm believer in God, although he never went to church. When making decisions, he told me to consider what Jesus would do. Mostly, my childhood feelings about God were rooted in fear. His judgmental, punishing ways scared me. When I was old enough, I washed my hands of it all. It was freeing to leave behind beliefs that had bordered on cruel and fantastical.

In my early thirties, I went to dine out with my husband and another couple. The restaurant was busy and noisy, since the tables were close together. Across from me, our friend Stan was telling a story, and I was paying attention. Then a strange silence came over the room, as if all sound had been drained away. I looked around, but my friends weren't reacting, and no one else seemed to notice the change in the sound level.

At that point, four words came into my head intrusively, unlike anything I'd experienced up to that point—*God is watching you.* The four words came as a complete thought, not one word at a time. I was stunned at the way such a deep silence preluded the message and the dramatic deliverance of the words, as if someone or something wanted to make sure I noticed them. I asked myself why those particular words were spoken to me.

Over the following weeks, I thought about this event constantly. I tried to write it off as nothing but my imagination, yet at the same time, that explanation didn't feel true. As the days passed, I began to feel reverent about the voice, humbled, and blessed at what it had said. If something greater than me had tried to get my attention, was I going to ignore it and keep that door firmly closed?

I decided to ask some questions of this voice. Whatever this was, I needed it to prove its existence to myself. I wasn't going to welcome something I didn't understand into my life without taking precautions. I started by sitting quietly and envisioning myself in a protective white light, saying the Lord's Prayer. I silently requested of the voice something along the lines of, "Who are you and what do you want?" I explained my reticence and that I would appreciate a very clear response, because I didn't think the voice was real.

At the end of my questions, an incredible wave of love and bliss washed through me. I'd never felt anything as sudden and as beautiful. I couldn't ignore this, whatever it was. Still, I had doubts, and for weeks I repeated this meditative process. Finally, after one especially beautiful meditation, I was convinced the voice and the subsequent waves of bliss were something other than my imagination.

As I continued to meditate in this way, my life perspective was forever changed. The stresses of day-to-day life were dissolved. I became more forgiving, compassionate, patient, understanding, respectful, and loving, probably because this was how I was being treated by this presence.

This began a quest for me to learn more about the origin of this voice and how it brought with it such deep feelings of love. Eventually I joined a Fellowship where I learned how to go deeper into meditation. These years of my life were my most even-minded, motivated, and euphoric. My experiences during this time were deeply personal, and I shared them with very few people. I won't defend them or try to prove their existence. I don't have the words to describe whatever it was that came to me. I believe it was something other than me. For want of a label, this profound something that showed me how to get closer to love for myself and others, I chose to call God. With those words—*God is watching you*—I came as close to Him or Her as I have ever been.

Typically, documented encounters with the Divine describe the event as coming unexpectedly with no forewarning, usually outdoors along a roadside or inside a mountain cave. There is little or no physical detail of the Divine One's appearance. Instead, the Divine is experienced as a massive, overwhelming Presence that shakes the soul of the seeker and changes his view of the world ever after, or in some cases even shapes a grand religion. The Christian mystics seem most often to experience the divine in personal terms of a love relationship with the person of Jesus Christ, while in other religions, it seems more of a non-human loving presence. In most cases, before the divine encounter, the seekers have a connection with a religious view of life—if not with an established religion, at least with humanitarian principles for living with others. Occasionally, a sinner will be blessed by God with a divine encounter, resulting in him or her being elevated in later years to the status of a saint.

As I worked my way through the commentaries on the sacred texts, it dawned on me that the key spiritual figures whose views formed the foundation for the three dominant monotheistic religions (Christianity, Islam, and Judaism) were men—Jesus Christ, the Prophet Muhammad, and Yahweh being the principal conduits for God's word. Succeeding sages, commentators, and prophets drew up foundational scriptures for each religion—the Bible, the Torah, and the Qur'an. None of these formulators of divine guidelines were female, which explains in good part why women were denied access to positions of power within the religious hierarchies. Occasionally, a few women rose to spiritual prominence through their visions and raptures, said to be gifts from God, as was the case with St. Hildegard of Bingen and St. Teresa of Avila. But in essence,

these women were riffing on and extending the theologies originally promulgated by men. This isn't to say that men got it all
wrong, but for the independent seeker, it's well to note the one-
sided version of religious orthodoxies drawn up by men with
little or no input from women.

It seems rather narrow minded to create a spiritual life
through the lens of one sex. But that is what has happened
around the world. Religious orthodoxies everywhere have been
formulated solely by the male sex. The consequence has been
cruel, life-denying injustices for many women over all times
and in all places, to the point where opinions such as "Women
have no souls" and "Women are not worthy of being sources
of God's words" are spoken of and accepted in some religious
quarters. I wonder what the history of religious conflicts would
look like today if women had been listened to as crucial and
equal manifestations of the human spirit. Would the torture
and killings of the Spanish Inquisition have happened? Would
the bloody Christian crusades to militarily win back the Holy
Land from the Muslims have happened? The list of religious
wars is a long and brutal one. Would the female tendency to
avoid violent conflicts have made the world a more peaceable
place? At least the male tendency to use catastrophic wars to
solve disagreements might have been dampened down.

Reading my way to God has proven to be the undertaking of a
lifetime with no end in sight. I can't remember the titles of all the
books I've read over the last five decades, but I clearly recall the
cumulative joy of absorbing the mind-expanding knowledge found
within their pages. There were never enough free hours in the day
to fit in all that I wanted to read. Most of my spiritual reading was
squeezed in while riding the commuter train, over solo lunches,
or at night before sleep overtook me. These books that now line

the bookcases in my home are markers of the trail I blazed in my search for a glimpse of the divine. I wrote this poem as a testimony to the depth of my compulsion to continue reading books:

Books I Want to Read

The list of books I want to read
grows longer and more various
as chapters of my life speed past.

Sometimes I try to read
three books at a time
but somehow nothing sticks.

I put these three away for another day
and then I find two new ones
that make my mind purr with pleasure.

My bookcase grows and grows
with the remnants of my travels
each shelf marking the passing of a decade.

For my funeral I have requested
a second plot, a second casket
to hold the books, I still want to read.[11]

---

11. Linda Cassidy, *Inland Waterways: Poems From a Peaceable Kingdom* (Mississauga, Ontario: In Our Words Inc., 2010), 79.

THREE:

THE WAY OF YOGA

THREE:

THE WAY OF YOGA

discovered the spiritual discipline of yoga in 1971. I was thirty years old and living in Adelaide, Australia, with my husband and two infant sons. At the time, I was working part-time in the Barr Smith Library at the University of Adelaide, while my husband consulted as an engineer on the South Australian natural gas network. In the afternoons I was in the habit of tuning into a TV program to watch an instructor perform an exercise regime called yoga. I followed along with the instructor and noticed afterward my body felt more energized and, at the same time, more relaxed.

Five years later I returned to the Toronto region, where I worked downtown in a coordinating office for academic libraries in Ontario and Quebec. One day an advertisement in our suburban newspaper caught my eye. It promoted yoga classes to be held weekly in the basement of the local Masonic lodge. Here I met a most inspiring yoga instructor named Isobel Athey. She would prove to be my portal into a spiritual world that for a period eased my yearning for Something-Other-Than.

At the time Isobel was in her mid-fifties, barely five feet tall and petite, in contrast to my five-foot-nine frame. Her hair was completely white, yet despite her age, Isobel radiated the spirit of a young woman. She spoke in quiet, soothing tones that erased any lingering resistance to her instructions. Years of yoga practice had rendered her body as flexible and strong as that of a woman in her twenties. She carried herself with a youthful grace that reminded me of Audrey Hepburn, my favourite movie star at the time.

Hour-long yoga lessons with Isobel came to be a regular feature of my week. In those days I was living the householder's life at full throttle with a husband and two sons, aged seven and eight, as well as a professional career in a consortium of university libraries. Two hours of the day were spent commuting into Toronto. While my career was exciting and I loved my family dearly, at times the pace was overwhelming, and I yearned for a still space where I could just be. Yoga offered me that space.

Every Tuesday evening at 5:20 I took the commuter train from downtown to my home in the suburb of Oakville. After tossing together a quick meal for the family, I headed off to the Masonic Hall for my 7:00 p.m. session of yoga. Isobel had an enthusiastic group of students, mostly women, with men making occasional appearances. Isobel opened each session with a brief presentation on the history and benefits of yoga. I learned yoga was not just a way to keep your body slim and flexible but came with an ancient and comprehensive philosophy of mind and spirit. She spoke often of her yoga teacher and spiritual guide. She called him Gurudev. He lived in an ashram in the Blue Mountains of Pennsylvania, northwest of Philadelphia. She had been initiated as his disciple and given the name *Kaveri*, a Sanskrit word meaning "she-who-has-a-body-made-of-water." She often said that to be in Gurudev's presence was a unique experience, and we should consider visiting the ashram to experience the phenomenon for ourselves.

In the 1970s, the science of yoga was just beginning to be noticed by the popular culture of North America. In the

1960s, several East Indian spiritual teachers, calling themselves gurus, arrived on the shores of North America in response to a spiritual gap created by the declining influence of orthodox Christianity. These gurus brought with them an ancient and venerable lineage of rituals and spiritual disciplines with the aim to bring harmony between mind and body, leading eventually to the union of individual consciousness with that of Universal Consciousness. In the beginning, the strangeness of yoga to the Western mind caused suspicion. I remember my father expressing concern at my involvement in this "heathen cult."

The success of these early yoga practitioners in transplanting an Eastern spiritual tradition to the West with its predominantly Christian populace was an amazing phenomenon that endures to this day, albeit in a more commercialized form. Something in the yogic tradition spoke to the hearts and minds of educated, middle-class people in the West. The primary attraction for me, and I imagine for others, was yoga's focus on the body and the direct experience of changed consciousness. I wasn't sure what harmony between mind and body felt like, not to mention what it meant to be in union with a rarified something called Universal Consciousness. My body responded in a unique way to the variety of yoga exercises called asanas. My muscles and solar plexus hummed in a relaxed state of contentment unfamiliar to me until this point. At the same time, I felt a surge of energy move throughout my entire body, an energy that empowered me both physically and mentally.

Later, I learned that yoga and Christianity have divergent views on the role played by the body in entering a state of spiritual grace. For the yoga practitioner, the presence of God resides within the body and as such is to be revered as the ground and temple for union with God. In contrast, Christian theology considers the body an obstacle to merging with the divine; only through a relationship with his son, Jesus Christ, can the seeker come home to God. For this reason, the strictly faithful are instructed to control the body through practices that mortify its passions; sex is to be indulged in solely for the procreation of children conceived within a once-in-a-lifetime marriage. This belief informs the controversial Catholic prohibition against birth control.

The practice of yoga begins with the care of the bodily temple through a series of asanas, breathing patterns, and dietary guidelines. These basic observances lead to meditation, the reading of sacred scripture, chanting, fasting, and serving as the disciple of a guru. In time, with the support of a guru and the steadfast practice of the yogic disciplines, the disciple may achieve the goal of liberation and enlightenment, known as samadhi.

At the time, I was very aware of news accounts exposing the darker side of these guru holy men who succumbed to the worst aspects of Western materialism. Some of them set up ashrams with devoted followers (devotees) who gave them sex in gratitude for spiritual insight, and donated money for the purchase of fancy cars and luxury homes. I felt uncomfortable when Isobel spoke of the "special" nature of being in Gurudev's presence, what a blessing it was to listen to him. The news reports combined with my natural skepticism of worshipping anyone as though he (in most cases the revered gurus were men) was a god incarnate caused alarm bells to go off in my mind. After all, this guru person was a human being like me. I couldn't see what his physical presence could offer me.

While I shrugged off Isobel's effusive praise of Gurudev, I recognized she was a superb instructor—humble and kind, two characteristics I admired in a spiritual teacher. Besides, she wasn't preachy about Gurudev. She simply acknowledged his role in her life, and she didn't go on about it in an evangelical manner. One day she told the class the ashram was offering a special weekend for first-timers at a reduced rate. She planned to drive down to Pennsylvania. Would anyone like to join her? A couple of people in the class said they'd like to come. I'd had a very busy time at work, and I needed a break. What better way to get away for a while than go to a yoga retreat and ashram with friends? And one where a guru was in residence! What a great conversational gambit that would make over lunch at the office!

And so it happened, late one Friday afternoon in the fall of 1977, six years after my introduction to yoga on Australian television, I drove with Isobel and two of her other students east on Route 90 and south on Route 81 to the Blue Mountains of Pennsylvania and the ashram where I would meet a real-life guru. I remember a sense of elation. I was truly launched on my quest, no longer dependent on books.

We arrived at the ashram in the early evening. Located on 240 acres of forested land, the facility included a two-storey main building on the shore of a small lake and several lesser dwellings situated on opposite shores. As we entered the main building, drumbeats greeted us, accompanied by music from an instrument I didn't recognize. I later discovered it was a harmonium, created during the years of British rule in India. With one hand the musician fingered a miniature keyboard while reaching across the instrument to squeeze a bellows-like extension. The resulting sound was exotic and energetic, closely resembling that of a bagpipe.

We followed the drumbeats and the strains of the harmonium to a large room filled with people clapping and chanting to the tempo of the music. The room was in semi-darkness, the main illumination emanating from a raised dais where an East Indian man dressed in white sat on a large, upholstered chair, playing the harmonium set up on a small table before him. The long, wide room was carpeted with an intense apricot-coloured broadloom rug. No chairs, only small cushions arranged in regularly spaced rows. As the aroma of incense filled the air, people jumped about, clapping and chanting to the dervish-like music. The room, which was essentially a chapel, resounded with a magical charge of sound that engaged all my senses and caused my body to reverberate to the rhythms of the music.

Although I had listened to recordings of the sedate, free-flowing Gregorian chants of the Roman Catholic Church, these yogic chants were something very different. One didn't sit back and listen; one got up and joined in the strong, harmonious beat. The music filled me with a sensation of love and joy that made it impossible to deny my body's urge to join in the enchantment. At one point, a surge of sensation travelled up my spine, causing my upper body to jerk about in a mildly convulsive state. The devotees around me also appeared to be possessed by the same unseen energy. The music, the orange carpet, the emotional chanting, the ability to move about as an expression of joy—all came to me as a welcome contrast to the stiffness and formality of the wooden pews and stone floors of Protestant churches and Roman Catholic cathedrals.

I later learned this coming together of seekers to chant with the guru was called satsang, a Sanskrit word meaning the "coming together of the wise." Fervent singing and dancing are a part of the worship services of other religions such as the Quakers and the Black Baptist churches of the American South. For some reason, these practices seem to have been passed over by the mainstream Christian religions, both Catholic and Protestant.

For the rest of the weekend, I joined in the simple but pleasant life of the two hundred permanent ashram residents. We rose at 5:00 a.m. and walked or jogged along the paths in the surrounding woodlands. Jogging through the cold, predawn hours was another first-time experience for me, and not one I particularly relished.

Throughout the day, the chapel served as the focus of all our activities. We ate our meals there from trays while sitting cross-legged on the floor and participated in yoga classes and workshops. In the evening everyone gathered in the chapel for satsang. As guests, we slept inside sleeping bags laid out on thin foam mats on the broadloom; the ashram residents retired to small houses on the other side of the lake. It was lights-out at 9:30 p.m., which didn't fit in well with my night-owl habits, but it was probably wise considering our 5:00 a.m. rising.

Life that weekend at the ashram was stimulating yet calming, enjoyable yet emotionally turbulent. The food was strictly vegetarian, a profound switch in diet for me from my usual regime of steak, pork, and chicken with side portions of vegetables and a delicious dessert laced with sugar. It was a culinary revelation to discover that frozen peas and sliced carrots weren't the only options in a well-prepared vegetarian meal and that lentils, hummus, beans, brown rice, and millet could be reworked into tasty versions of protein to replace the ubiquitous sirloin steak. I tasted tofu for the first time, but its slightly rubbery texture and bland taste never won me over.

The ashram practice of ingesting dinner in complete silence was a revelation. Not having to make chit-chat throughout the meal left space and energy to focus on the subtle flavours of the food. The ashram called this change in our attitude "conscious eating." After a weekend living without chairs and tables, I viewed these household artifacts in my home as rather odd and unnecessary. Years later, when the ashram moved to larger quarters, we ate cafeteria-style with chairs and tables. I rather missed sitting on the floor to eat. It seemed more authentically spiritual and simple than sitting at a table.

I tried over the years to take on a vegetarian diet, which in the 1970s was considered an exotic way of eating. While I enjoyed the vegetarian meals at the ashram, I was never able to make the switch in my home cooking. I'd been raised to consider meat the centrepiece of a meal, and I could never let that mindset go.

The ashram ran a series of workshops and encounter sessions dealing with relationships and emotional blocks. We sat in dyads, cross-legged on the floor with our knees almost touching and our gazes interlocked with no expression. We were not supposed to offer up solutions to our partner's problems but just listen and bear witness to their emotional or spiritual pain. I reluctantly joined in a few of the dyads, but I wasn't keen on divulging my emotional wounds to strangers, or listening to their problems. Eventually, I perfected the art of sneaking out of the room before the dyads started. Whenever the workshop coordinator spoke the words "find a partner," I scurried off to the bathroom and stayed there until the workshop had moved on to other topics.

For me, the most dramatic and inspiring part of the day was satsang, where yoga, music, ritual, and chanting came together in a powerful dynamic. With no direct experience of Indian spiritual traditions, the significance of the rituals enacted around me and the images of the Hindu gods on the altar escaped me. I never took the time to learn about them. It was the rituals of light and dark and the musical vibrations that nurtured me at a deep level. The pantheon of Hindu gods seemed extraneous to all these wonders. In retrospect, I should have learned more about the cultural background of yoga to better comprehend its tenets.

The vigorous yoga classes were the star attraction at the ashram. Led by senior disciples, each session touched on a wide variety of classic yogic asanas and concluded with a delicious fifteen-minute relaxation that loosened every tense muscle in the body. The calming effect so stilled the racing mind, many practitioners fell asleep. These ashram-trained yoga instructors were the best I ever encountered. They brought a unique spiritual quality to their teaching, which I credit to their connection with the guru at the heart of the ashram—Yogi Amrit Desai or, as he was more affectionally called, Gurudev.

The reverential term Gurudev means "luminous guru," referring to the yoga master's subtle, inner light that shines from a place beyond the physical body. In the yogic tradition, the guru is considered a manifestation of God and the light of spiritual guidance.

When I met Gurudev for the first time that weekend in 1977, he was in his early forties, tall and lean with shining black hair that reached his shoulders. He had arrived in the United States twelve years earlier from the province of Gujarat in southern India, accompanied by his wife and three young children. He had been sent by his spiritual father, the great yoga master Swami Shri Kripalvanandji, to spread the truths of the ancient spiritual teachings of yoga to those in the West.

Gurudev's broad smile revealed a slight gap between his two front teeth, which somehow made his smile more infectious. He wore a long-sleeved, spotlessly white outfit that reached his ankles. When he entered the chapel for satsang, he glided down the aisle between the male and female disciples as though riding on smooth wheels. At the front of the gathering, he mounted a raised dais, where he sat on a silken cushion to play the harmonium and lead devotees and disciples in Sanskrit chants. My teacher, Isobel, was right about the dramatic effect of being in Gurudev's presence. My mind stopped darting about and focused with a sharp clarity on every word he spoke.

The highlight of a satsang with Gurudev was his lectures on yoga and meditation. He spoke English with a trace of an accent, but it was not the typical sing-song rhythm of most East Indians. His grasp of English grammar and idiom was fluent. When he delivered his lecture, or what Christians would call a sermon, he never referred to notes, even though he spoke for more than an hour at a time. Rarely hesitating or stumbling, his presentations on complex spiritual matters flowed seamlessly from him, settling deep within my consciousness. There were no loud rhetorical outbursts from him in the manner of Christian evangelicals. He articulated practical ways to live out the principles of yoga in a calm, clear, and down-to-earth manner. When asked how he could give such long lectures without notes, he claimed he never prepared a script. What we heard was spontaneous and came from a meditative place. Years later, I had the opportunity to transcribe recordings of his lectures. Only then did I become aware of pauses and repetitions in his speech. Perhaps being in his presence made the audience so at one with his energy that they heard him as he wished to be heard—every word exact and delivered without hesitation. The transcriptions confirmed what Gurudev told his followers—that he did not prepare a letter-perfect script beforehand.

Gurudev's guru, Swami Shri Kripalvanandji, whom he called Bapuji, meaning spiritual grandfather, came to live for a time at the ashram in the late 1970s and early 1980s. I joined him in satsang two years after my first visit to the ashram. Bapuji was an authentic spiritual seeker in the Hindu tradition, having lived a monk's existence since his youth. For twenty-two years he remained in complete silence, communicating with others only through writing words on a chalk slate. He wrote that he had surrendered his entire life to the Lord and that he had become addicted to sadhana. This intense inner discipline (sadhana) generated a forcefield of powerful energies within him that could be felt by those around him. His demeanour was one of joy, the level of joy that typically appears on the face of a very young child. The effect of being in his presence while he chanted and spoke was to root you to the spot, your mind and body utterly still. Gurudev also possessed this powerful level of energy, but Bapuji's was far more intense and seemed to travel throughout the ashram building.

On one occasion, Bapuji spoke at satsang for an hour in his native tongue of Gujarati. Usually, Gurudev translated his guru's words as he went along, but this time Bapuji didn't wait for the translation to catch up. The Master just kept on speaking. During the entire hour I sat cross-legged and motionless while he talked in a language that to me was utterly indecipherable. Although my intellect could make nothing of what he said, I did not become bored. My mind focused with laser sharpness on the sound of his voice and the sight of him sitting on the dais with Gurudev at his feet. I don't recall a single thought entering my mind. It remained clear and refreshed yet ready to jump into creative mode at any moment. Those who sat near me in the chapel also remained rooted to the spot, with no whispering or fidgeting.

This energy was a by-product of an ancient technique called Shakitpat, in which the divine essence in the Master is energetically transmitted to the deserving disciple. This technique, the sages claimed, caused a profound shift in the consciousness and energetic field in the disciple receiving it. Gurudev often told the story of his receiving Shaktipat from Bapuji and afterward having the divine energy (prana) within his body awaken and manifest by spontaneous postures, which propelled his mind into a deep meditative state. Like many East Indian gurus, Gurudev eventually developed his own modified version of yoga based on the timeless practices Bapuji taught him. He took the root of his guru's name, "Kripal," and created a brand of yoga he named "Kripalu Yoga: Meditation in Motion."

Gurudev demonstrated his spontaneous posture flow at his workshops. He began by kneeling in the centre of the room, encircled by the participants. For a few minutes he breathed slowly and deeply. Soon his eyes closed, and he entered a meditative state. Those watching also closed their eyes as they entered meditation. Then Gurudev's body began to stretch and move extremely slowly, while his eyes remained closed throughout. He would assume a series of horizontal yoga postures, each one blending into the previous ones, to the point where it became difficult to differentiate one posture from the other. His body moved like stalks of wheat in a field, set in motion by a gentle breeze. It was difficult, almost impossible, to view the entire posture flow, which lasted about forty-five minutes, as my eyes kept closing against my will and I would drop into a meditative state. Throughout the flow, everyone remained standing in complete silence. Without fail, my eyes would open at the precise moment Gurudev ended his posture flow.

Being able to perform a spontaneous posture flow was considered the pinnacle of achievement for Kripalu yoga students. I saw several senior disciples demonstrate a flow, but the aura from them was never as strong as it was with Gurudev. I certainly never attained this level of success, although on occasion during meditation my hands would move spontaneously through space in extreme slow motion. If I had consciously tried, I couldn't have made my hands move that slowly.

―――――――

My initial experiences at the ashram greatly encouraged me. I was tremendously excited at having found a spiritual tradition, Hinduism, with bone fide credentials that went back many centuries. I knew something was happening to me, but I couldn't say for certain what it was. Was I encountering God in some fashion? Perhaps my spiritual quest was only chasing after a dream, a fairy tale or myth created by early humans to assuage their fear and anxiety about the violent and dangerous world they inhabited. I was of a naturally skeptical frame of mind and well aware of the effects on one's thinking when part of a group. Groupthink was something I wanted to avoid at all costs. Yet I couldn't deny that my body, and to some extent my spirit, were responding to some force perceived as real. The energy moving about my body was similar to what I'd felt years before when my unborn child moved about in my womb. I mentioned this observation to Gurudev during a Q&A after one of his lectures. He smiled and said that something new was being born within me. I took his words to mean a new version of my inner self was in the process of coming into being.

After my first weekend, I took every opportunity to visit the ashram, which turned out to be once or twice a month. Even though my husband was completely capable and willing to look after our sons, I still felt a typical twinge of motherly guilt leaving my post as mother-in-chief on the weekends. I pushed the guilt aside; I was hot on the trail of spiritual enlightenment that, if it happened, would benefit the entire family.

I travelled the seven-hour trip to the ashram with other Kripalu yoga enthusiasts from the Toronto region. We would carpool for the drive south to the American border, giving our reason for entering the country as the visiting of friends. Not a word about going to an ashram, as such a statement might lead to a search of the car for cannabis or magic mushrooms. In the 1970s, governments were suspicious of religious cults, and for some people even yoga fell into that category. After crossing the border, with nothing exceptional in the scenery to distract us, we passed time by confessing our marital, religious, and addiction issues to each other. Giddy with anticipation of two days marinating in the high-voltage energy of the gurus, we opened ourselves to the possibility that our lives weren't the train wrecks we feared and our personal problems might be solvable. Many times, the car speeding toward the ashram was transformed into a confessional booth on wheels, lacking only the mediation of a priest.

One of my trips to the ashram was particularly memorable. Due to circumstances I can no longer recall, I travelled with two men—or brothers, as they were called in spiritual circles. One was a psychologist named Norman, and the other a psychiatrist named Stephen. They were lively companions, full of stories and interesting observations about Gurudev and how his spiritual power helped them in their professional work with patients. Unfortunately, both Norman and Stephen were addicted to cigarettes and smoked non-stop in the car. I was intensely sensitive to cigarette smoke, but since I was a guest in their car, I couldn't object. I rolled down the window every few miles and gulped in fresh air. Norman and Stephen apologized but claimed it was impossible for them not to smoke. What, I wondered, would they do at the ashram, where smoking was forbidden? Obviously, these two healers of the human psyche were in the grip of a full-fledged obsessive addiction. By way of explaining their addictions, they talked about the stress they lived under in their practices, which made them vulnerable to absorbing the emotional stress of their patients into their own psyche. They claimed the human body registers our unresolved emotions as tension in the muscles and brain. One of the reasons Norman and Stephen visited the ashram was to receive body massages that could dissipate the tensions passed on to them by their patients. It sounded to me like a form of exorcism to drive out their evil spirits or demons.

A physical link between the body and repressed emotions? This was a new concept for me. At that point in my life, I believed emotions originated in the gut, kicked up a storm of tears and maybe angry shouting before vanishing into the ether. End of story. To believe emotions lingered behind, buried in our bones and muscles, seemed a bridge too far. However, my resistance softened the next day when I overheard Norman hollering like a banshee while undergoing a massage. Maybe there was something about this body-emotion link after all. Immediately, I booked a whole-body massage for myself.

My massage therapist quickly focused on my jawbone near my ears. Within minutes of applying a firm pressure with her fingers, I was convulsed with sobbing that could be heard in the next county. I was appalled at the scene I was creating. I didn't want to cry, and I didn't know what I was crying about. It was all very embarrassing. The therapist didn't seem bothered or surprised by my personal drama. Her intuition, she told me, had immediately guided her fingers to the tight muscles in my jawline, which signified the repression of things I'd wanted to say over the years but never did. What those unspoken words were about—well, that was for me to discover.

Later, a guest at the ashram told me of her son, who had been hurt as a young child in an accident. He ran home to her, his face covered in blood. When the mother saw his bloodied face, she wanted to cry out in horror but knew that would alarm her son even more. So she said nothing but went about wiping away the blood and comforting her child. For years afterward she suffered from gum disease and other dental issues. When she had a massage at the ashram the therapist, as in my case, focused on her jawline. Immediately she received a flashback of her son's face covered with blood. She began to sob very loudly, even though the incident with her son had happened many years earlier. I didn't have such a flashback to tell me what emotions I had suppressed, but I was now convinced of the connection between the body and the mind.

At the end of my weekend at the ashram, I stood in the parking lot as I prepared to return to Toronto in another car. Stephen walked up to me and handed me a small photograph of Gurudev in a silver frame. I was moved at having made a spiritual connection of sorts with this educated but still troubled man. I wondered how he and Norman had managed to handle their addiction over the weekend. I never saw my two healers of the psyche lurking outside the building for a smoke. Perhaps they snuck off into the woods for a quick drag.

Visiting the ashram opened me to participation in Hindu rituals. While unlike anything I had witnessed in Christian churches, I felt a great affinity for these traditions and the extensive dynasty of Hindu gods and goddesses that came with them. This immediate acceptance and enjoyment of the Hindu spiritual life made me almost believe in reincarnation for a few moments. Perhaps in a previous life I had lived as a Hindu woman, and these rituals were familiar to me at some cosmic level.

The satsang held every evening was the primary choreographed gathering. Gurudev opened with a series of chants followed by a lecture on aspects of the spiritual life, including the relationship between guru and disciple, life as a play of energy, the release of emotional attachments, and the physical and mental disciplines required to attain enlightenment. The aroma of incense, which I had rejected in my visit to Saint Joseph's Oratory many years earlier, was now a source of great pleasure and helped deepen my meditation. After the lecture, the devotees asked Gurudev questions about their struggles on the spiritual path. The satsang closed with a ceremony of light known as arti that was sung and performed with reverence, adoration, and meditative awareness.

Arti is one of the most important and popular ceremonies of the Hindu faith. It is sung while a disciple or priest waves a lighted wick before sacred images of Hindu deities. The prayer is accompanied by musical instruments, including the harmonium, drums, handheld bells, and sometimes a conch shell. After the prayer, the priest or a disciple passes among the gathering with the lighted wick. The devotees hold their hands briefly over the flame and then pass them over their eyes and head in a sweeping motion. In this way, it is believed the devotees share in the blessings of the gods, which have been infused within the flames. While I felt a bit awkward performing the gestures of arti, I had to admit the ceremony was not unlike the moment of transubstantiation in the Roman Catholic mass when the wine and wafer mysteriously and metaphorically turn into the body and blood of Christ.

I found myself emotionally affected by the arti ceremony, especially during the concluding prayer, when music and chanting penetrated my being, bathing me in an aura of sweet love that moved me to tears of joy. Yet I didn't understand a word of what was being sung. I concluded this soulful effect had nothing to do with "knowing" in the intellectual sense but came from a place of pure feeling. What a contrast to the effect of the sonorous, heavy prayers sung in the Protestant United Church, which conjured up for me intimations of suffering, anguish, and eventual death. The Hindu drums and harmonium celebrated the joy of life in its drama of here and now.

At various points in the satsang rituals, the entire gathering of seekers dropped to their knees and touched their foreheads to the floor. To my amazement, the first time I bowed in this fashion it felt so right, so appropriate. I had no idea to what I was bowing— truth, God, Gurudev, my soul? Maybe life itself. I had no idea; it just felt freeing and liberating. Previously, I had associated bowing with subservience. In the late 1970s, the women's rights campaign sparked by Gloria Steinem's *Ms. Magazine* and Betty Friedan's book *The Feminine Mystique* was in full swing, and I was in complete accord with their views. At that time, the through-line for the lives of liberated young women was to stand on your own two feet economically, emotionally, and professionally. To bow down, especially in front of a male guru, was understandably treasonous to anyone who participated in the women's liberation movement. I recall a young woman guest who approached three of us at the end of satsang which included much bowing.

"Why are you bowing to that man?" she asked us in an angry tone.

"We're not bowing to him as a man," one of us replied. (It might have been me.) "We're bowing to what he stands for—the Divine."

The young woman shook her head vehemently. "No, you think he is a God. But he's only a man. What are you thinking? How can you lower yourself so? What do you think we are fighting for?"

"We are bowing to the divine in him, as there is the divine within us," replied another one of my friends. It might even have been me who spoke.

"No, you're wrong to bow down to anyone, especially to any man." Then she walked off.

Intellectually, I understood her perspective. A year earlier I wouldn't have bowed on my knees to anyone. But bowing now felt the right thing to do. I wasn't bowing to Gurudev but to a "something" moving through him. This was an instance of following my quest with my heart as well as my intellect.

Other new terms besides satsang and arti entered my vocabulary: "Jai Bhagwan," or "Namaste," a Hindi version of an ancient Sanskrit greeting meaning "I honour the light within you" or "I bow to the divine within you." This greeting is spoken with the hands held together above the heart in the prayer position. It's most often used as a respectful greeting between teacher and pupil. Yoga postures became "yoga asanas," and breathing exercises were referred to as "pranayama." Overarching these new words was the universal sound represented by the Sanskrit word "OM," pronounced in three parts—ahh-ooh-mmm. When spoken correctly, the sound reverberates throughout the body and mind, creating an alert mental state ideal for meditation. The vibrations are most keenly felt when spoken in unison with others.

Mantras, the repetition of a sacred phrase to support meditation, are a feature in yoga as they are in Roman Catholicism and Buddhism. "Holy Mary, Mother of God" is a popular one for Catholics, as is "Om mani padme hum" in the Buddhist tradition. At the Kripalu ashram, both disciples and guests chanted "Om Namo Bhagavate Vasudevaya," one of the more popular Hindu mantras praising the supreme god. It roughly translates as "Om and Salutations to the divine One who dwells in all." Another translation I found was "Let thy word be done, Oh Lord, not mine." In fact, the literal meaning of a mantra is not all that critical; it's the sound that is said to possess mystical qualities. I found it very calming to repeat the guru mantra silently or out loud. Since the mind can't comprehend the words, it isn't able to free-associate and generate a host of idle thoughts and disturbing fears. A mantra spoken enthusiastically for a time can block out external noise, which is why mantras should not be spoken while driving a car or performing any process requiring mental vigilance. I use my mantra to this day to block negative, non-productive thoughts. And it still works.

About a year after my initial visit to the ashram, I began to entertain the notion of becoming a disciple. There was no pressure from Gurudev or his disciples to undergo a formal initiation. Any resistance to taking this step came from me. I felt a bit leery of stepping into the role of a disciple, as this term was associated in my mind with the original followers of Jesus Christ. To call myself a disciple seemed sacrilegious and not in keeping with who I considered myself to be. I didn't want to come off as a phony to others and, most importantly, to myself.

In addition, the reputation of modern-day gurus was not the best. Throughout the 1960s and 1970s, stories appeared frequently in the media of Indian gurus who took advantage of the financial generosity of their disciples to fund a lavish lifestyle hardly in keeping with the simplicity they preached. This financial abuse was often the downfall of gurus. It would begin innocently enough with the need faced by every spiritual community—how to finance the continued existence of the community. It takes money to set up and maintain the infrastructure of the organization, which includes buildings, property, and staff. One cannot live on the spirit alone. How a community generates this needed revenue can lead to dodgy finances. Kripalu appeared to survive financially through offering yoga classes and presenting workshops on how to integrate aspects of yoga into everyday life. The price of the programs included room and board. The money charged was not at all excessive and, in my view, the value received far exceeded what I paid out. During the time I visited, the ashram ran fundraising efforts to elicit income beyond that generated from the yoga programs. I heard that several wealthy disciples made substantial donations, although I never spotted any Mercedes or Cadillacs parked on the ashram property.

I dove into reading about the role of a disciple in the Hindu religion. The Kripalu ashram had published several booklets on yoga and the nuances of the guru-disciple relationship. The disciple concept does not sit well in the Western way of life, as it suggests an extreme form of subservience to someone else's ideas. In the West, the term most often used to describe a strong non-romantic relationship between two people is "mentor," applied mainly in business and politics. The terms "priest" and "parishioner" come closer to the guru-disciple relationship, but they are much less intense. The challenge of uncovering the God within is a difficult one. The sacred texts speak of achieving enlightenment as a process of walking on a razor's edge. The seeker needs help on this path. Only a guru who has gone through the spiritual fires can advise and support the disciple as he or she comes closer to the divine energy of God within.

In yogic scriptures, the relationship between guru and disciple is described as one of intense, all-inclusive love. An ancient prayer to the guru says:

> Thou art my mother, my father thou art,
> Thou art my brother, my friend thou art,
> Thou art my knowledge, my wealth thou art,
> Thou art my all, my god of Gods thou art.[12]

In a booklet published in the mid-1970s, the Kripalu ashram characterized the nature of the guru-disciple relationship in the following manner:

> Throughout the relationship the guru never judges, never is displeased with a disciple's progress. He is completely familiar—and hence accepting of—all the private domains of human feeling and experience—and encourages the "taking out of the garbage" without being overcome by its odour. The path of kundalini yoga is the path of purification,

---

12. Yogi Amrit Desai, *Guru and Disciple: A Relationship of Love* (Sumneytown, Pa.: Kripalu Yoga Ashram, 1975), 45.

and Gurudev's love enables us to clean out the stables without giving way to negativity. Behind the scenes he guides the disciple safely through all stages of growth on the spiritual path.[13]

While the love between guru and disciple can resemble romantic love in some ways, ideally the guru should not become attached to the disciple to the point of manipulating him or her for the guru's advantage, whether it be for sex or for money. It's an extremely difficult feat for the guru to pull off, as he can become trapped in his own ego projections, which can lead to the development of an inappropriate relationship between guru and disciple.

I still had one other issue to settle in my mind. After a year of participating in satsangs in which spiritual seekers, including myself, twitched and danced around as though afflicted by a form of palsy, I still didn't understand what was going on. Anyone watching these reactions from the sidelines might rightly be alarmed and wonder if these people were suffering a mental disorder. From inside the experience, I could say it was enjoyable and exhilarating. While I might act in an uncontrollable manner, I was always objectively aware of my surroundings and never felt in danger. I could have stepped back from the music and chanting at any point if I so wished.

Gurudev was obviously the source of this strange energy. He could bring its physical manifestations to an immediate stop by slowing down the tempo of the chanting and modulating his voice. I researched the literature on the source of these physical effects and learned that similar types of responses occur in other religions. In Hinduism, this divine energy, called "kundalini," plays a significant

---

13. Rajendra, *Journey to the New Age: An Introduction to Life at Kripalu Yoga Ashram* (Sumneytown, Pa: Kripalu Yoga Fellowship, 1976), 26.

role in an individual's path to enlightenment. It's reputed to lie coiled, serpent-like, at the base of each person's spine. The goal of the asanas, meditation, and breathing exercises is to raise this energy up the seeker's spine until it reaches the crown of the head, where lies the highest peaks of spiritual enlightenment. A person who attains this level is said to have attained samadhi, or cosmic consciousness.

Through Divine Will and proper training, a guru master can stir up this latent kundalini power in a deserving disciple through a process called Shaktipat. The transfer of this spiritual energy opens an inner door in the disciple that enables him or her to experience a tremendous amount of love for the guru. This is the origin of the intense love felt between disciple and guru. Managing this divine energy is very challenging and requires the guru to guide the disciple through the dangers. In satsang, Gurudev often spoke of how the gift of kundalini had been given to him in this manner by his guru, Bapuji. A yogic prayer gives an insight into how this divine energy is perceived by both guru and disciple:

> I worship the Divine Light.
> I worship all that is holy forever and beyond
> In infinite bliss and infinite grace.
> I worship the light transmitted from Guru to disciple.
> I worship the Light Divine
> That is God within all and everything.[14]

While all this information was very strange and esoteric to me, I felt reassured that the pedigree for this view of spiritual enlightenment was thousands of years old and aspects of it existed in other religions. I realized I only understood fragments of the spiritual context in which Gurudev manifested

---

14. Rajarshi Muni, *Light from Guru to Disciple* (Sumneytown, Pa.: Kriplau Yoga Ashram, 1974), XV.

his powers. But I was intrigued and excited to start out on this journey with his help. Becoming a disciple seemed the next logical step in my quest for Something-Other-Than. I would not let my ignorance stop me from moving on in my quest.

And so it happened in the spring of 1977, in a small house in the Perkiomen Valley of Pennsylvania, I was initiated as a disciple of Yogi Amrit Desai, disciple of Swami Shri Kripalvananda, himself a disciple of Swami Pranavanandji, Lord Lakulish, the twenty-eighth incarnation of Lord Shiva. Yogi Desai gave me and the other initiates a spiritual name. Mine was "Avani," the Sanskrit word meaning "the Earth." It connotes authenticity and an aura of warmth, fortitude, and generosity.

Becoming a disciple did not affect how I participated in my family and professional lives. I didn't move into the ashram or seek a secluded mountain top to meditate. When I told my husband I wanted to become a disciple, I could tell by his body language that he wasn't happy about it. It must have been a shock to him. During our four years of courtship and twelve years of marriage, I had never shown any religious or spiritual leanings. He only asked that I not neglect the family, which I would never do and never did. Our family was the rock of my existence. Unlike many husbands who strongly resented their wives becoming disciples of a man, my husband never complained, although, in retrospect, he wasn't overtly encouraging. I enjoyed my professional career as an information consultant and technical writer. Nothing changed there. I continued to relish the excitement of the new field of information technology.

One unexpected challenge of discipleship was to adjust to my new Sanskrit name. Providing a disciple with a Sanskrit name is a traditional act that binds guru and disciple in a spiritual lineage. For the disciple, taking a name from the guru represents a spiritual rebirth. I'm not sure whether Gurudev personally chose a name for each initiate. I presume he and his senior disciples chose an appropriate name reflective of our answers to questions in the application form we filled in to become disciples. I like to think Gurudev chose my name because it reflected my passion for gardening. Even so, it took me quite a while to respond to the name Avani. Over the years I have met only one other disciple with the same name.

I kept my identity as a disciple restricted to the tightly knit community of other devotees and yoga enthusiasts in my life. With one exception, nobody in my workplace knew I was a disciple. I went about my daily life clutching this amazing secret to my heart—I am a disciple, I hold the secret to life, I will never be ill again. This magical thinking was a by-product of the popular culture in the 1960s and 1970s, when the alternative health community believed that if you ate the right things, meditated, did yoga postures, and had the occasional coffee enema, you wouldn't get sick. This illusion evaporated years later when Gurudev's wife, who lived at the centre of this magical, inspiring world of yoga, was diagnosed with cancer and eventually died. Most disciples were shocked. I wasn't the only one who thought having a guru and practising yoga would protect me from cancer, maybe even death.

The Toronto chapter of the Kripalu Yoga Fellowship met for satsang every Sunday morning in rented premises. Those musically inclined played drums, finger cymbals, and harmonium as accompaniment to the chanting. In Gurudev's absence, we listened to tapes of his discourses. Even his voice alone resonated with us. In our role as disciples, we had a dress code of sorts, which was encouraged but not rigorously enforced. Devotees and disciples dressed entirely in white, even Gurudev. Only his guru, Swami Shri Kripalvananda (Bapuji), wore orange robes reminiscent of the bareheaded young men in orange trousers frequently seen at the time in Canadian airports, chanting the mantra "Hare Krishna, Hare Krishna, Hare, Hare" while handing out literature and proselytizing the Hare Krishna way of life. These oddly-dressed persons were the public face of what people considered to be a sect. Somehow, the orange robe when worn by Bapuji in accordance with Hindu tradition seemed to me entirely appropriate. Many of the sisters went the extra mile and wore white saris because it was rumoured this style of Indian dress pleased Gurudev. I never wore a sari because it felt false to who I was, as though I was dressing up for a costume party. Instead, like many others, I elected to wear white slacks and a matching turtleneck.

The indispensable accoutrement for all disciples was a string of 108 brown beads called a mala and worn around the neck. Mala beads were similar in intent to the Roman Catholic rosary, serving as an aid to focus the mind during meditation. Starting at the guru bead, the one bead that stood out from the others, the devotee drew each bead over the index finger with the thumb while saying the guru mantra *Om Namo Bhagavate Vasudevaya*. As I prepared to meditate with the mala, I imagined how my Roman Catholic grandparents might react to the sight of their heretical granddaughter practising the rosary ritual within the precincts of this heathen cult.

Gurudev advocated the practice of Brahmacharya, the regulation of the energy of the senses. All religious traditions, he said, teach that celibacy is necessary to transform the psyche by channelling the human energies to spiritual ends. Unmarried residents of the ashram were asked to refrain from sexual activities. I knew from questions asked by the brothers at satsang that this principle of celibacy was difficult for them to observe. As part of their exceptionally healthy lifestyle, the asanas and breathing techniques had the effect of heightening their sexual drive. Gurudev's advice to the brothers was to meditate and practise calming breath control. I never heard the resident sisters voice problems with an overabundance of sexual energy, but I suspect female modesty was at work here, especially in the presence of a male guru. For a time, I experienced a heightened sexual awareness, especially while performing the asanas. I don't recall if breathing exercises dimmed the surges of sensation. I only know my lascivious thoughts gradually faded away on their own.

Meditation, a critical aspect of yoga practice, did not come easily to me, especially when I meditated alone. It was much easier to calm the mind when sitting with a group of fellow seekers. The spiritual auras of each devotee spilled over to the others in the group, heightening the power available to everyone. I never had any profound revelations during my meditations. Sometimes my lower arms and fingers tingled, and my hands moved almost imperceptibly through space. This motion didn't occur consciously; rather, some other force was guiding my arms and hands. I also experienced the act of reading differently. The meaning and resonance of individual words pierced my consciousness in ways they hadn't before. Something was happening internally but at a very subtle level. And then, one day my spirit burst forth through the medium of poetry and I discovered another path toward Something-Other-Than. I had discovered "The Way of Poetry," a critical stage in my quest which I'll cover in the next chapter.

━━━━━━━━

I kept the nature of my spiritual practices to myself, even within the family. Of course, it was no secret I was attending yoga classes when I left after dinner dressed in my whites with a yoga mat tucked under one arm. Weekends at the ashram were planned well in advance. But I didn't discuss the principles of yoga with my husband or sons. Growing up, Fraser had been exposed to the missionary zeal of two aunts who enthusiastically subscribed to Christianity as extolled through the agency of the Anglican Church. The aunts gave him a family Bible in his teens, but the religious seed did not take root in him. He never expressed any interest in what I was learning and, if truth be told, I was happy not to have to explain things I still didn't quite comprehend. My new-found seed of spiritual belief was very tender and easily blighted by skepticism.

Our sons were too young to grasp much about yoga and what it might represent in anyone's life. Recently, I asked my eldest son what he thought at the time about my going to the ashram and wearing all-white clothing. He shrugged. "It was just something you did, Mom."

Not wanting to impose religious symbols on Fraser and the boys when it was not their choice to practise yoga, I created a space for meditation inside a walk-in closet in the spare bedroom, which had the advantage of a window at one end that looked out at a good-sized maple tree. I set up a plywood altar underneath the window with a framed photograph of Gurudev, two small votive candles, and an incense holder. My meditation cushion—a blue, velveteen pillow about three inches high— was positioned in front of the altar, where I sat cross-legged during meditation. It was in this closeted spot that I took my first steps in meditation and became slightly familiar with what praying might feel like.

One time when Gurudev was visiting the Toronto Kripalu Yoga Centre, I took Fraser and our two sons to satsang. They observed the full-blown arti rituals with music, chanting, and a discourse from the guru himself. Would the presence of the guru have the same effect on them as it had on me? Or would they think me crazy to indulge in this weird yoga thing? I can't recall them asking me a question or expressing any opinion positive or negative about the ritual, the music, or what Gurudev had to say. They just watched the ceremonial gathering and then we returned home.

My family's seeming indifference to what had transpired at satsang gave me a few moments of doubt. Was I completely wrong about this path? Had I been taken in by a spiritual charlatan? Should I stop doing yoga? I pushed away these thoughts. I was happy with my experience of yoga. I couldn't be guided by the opinion of others who had no background in what I was attempting. In retrospect, I wished I'd pressed my husband and sons for some opinion or tried to better explain to them the yogic traditions. I wanted to bestow on our children the comfort of a strong (although not extreme) spiritual view, but I had none to offer them. I was unsure of myself and still seeking my way. While we never attended church as a family, I believe we passed on to our sons a sense of right and wrong and showing by example the importance of kindness in dealing with others. I have watched them live these spiritual values in their lives without a formal religious upbringing.

In my professional life, I revealed my discipleship to only one person—my boss. Ralph was a particularly charismatic man with the soul of an artist and a strong attraction to the icons of Eastern Orthodox Christianity. He held an art degree in painting, but he had put aside his art career to become a professional librarian to better support his family. I was one of the five librarians he supervised as Director of the Office of Library Coordination for Ontario universities. Around the time I became a disciple, Ralph was in the grips of a mid-life crisis brought on by illness and the breakdown of his thirty-year marriage. Over lunch one day I told him about the ashram and how what I was learning from Gurudev was changing my way of thinking and being. He wanted to meet Gurudev and see for himself what it was like to be in his presence.

Soon after, Ralph joined me on a weekend workshop at the ashram, where Bapuji made one of his rare appearances at satsang, breaking his long years of silence to speak to the disciples. Afterward, Ralph seemed more relaxed and told me he was strongly affected by Bapuji's presence. Within a few months he had recovered his high spirits, resigned his position in the Office of Library Coordination, and returned to his art career, going on to hold several exhibits of his artwork. During this transition, Ralph told me that going to the ashram and absorbing the mysterious energy fields surrounding the two gurus had reached into the core of his psyche and freed him from his inner turmoil. He claimed Gurudev had saved his life.

My life as a disciple of Yogi Desai lasted for almost fifteen years. It beautifully complemented my family and professional lives, providing a bulwark against the few difficult times. Moreover, it offered me the company of other spiritual seekers, where friendships could form for reasons deeper than those in the world of work. I attended satsangs, visited the ashram, and tried to develop my own practice of asanas and meditation. It was difficult to maintain consistency, and I relied on the company of other seekers to keep going. It's almost impossible to create a whole new spiritual order in your soul entirely on your own.

While I was strongly attracted to the spiritual life, I never wanted to live the life of a nun or a recluse. I looked on my spiritual life as a golden thread woven amongst the bright tapestry of raising a family and pursuing professional ambitions. My daily existence was a good life, to be cherished and not shunned, even to pursue the supreme ambition—Something-Other-Than. The spiritual threads could become sparse at times, but I persisted and did not break the golden thread.

In the early 1990s, the family moved to Nova Scotia for three years. During that time, I received a letter from the Kripalu Yoga Fellowship informing me of the resignation of Yogi Desai as spiritual director of Kripalu. Inside was a letter from Gurudev admitting to inappropriate sexual contact with five women residents of the ashram. He did not try to explain or justify his behaviour; it was simply wrong and inappropriate, and he was entirely to blame.

I couldn't believe what I was reading. Quickly, my shock turned to disbelief, then anger. How could Gurudev be so foolish as to indulge in the cliché of clichés common to so many male gurus—sleeping with their young female disciples? I had expected he might stumble over some fine moral point, but to come to grief over such an obvious slip-up as adultery verged on pathetic. And not just one woman—after all, one woman could be a one-time lapse, a *cri de coeur*—but he admitted to sleeping with five women over fifteen years. In time, I realized this compulsiveness around sexual activity can present an obstacle for male practitioners of yoga. An aspect of yoga called Tantra yoga provides techniques for raising human energy or prana to an orgasmic level of consciousness. I noticed that doing yoga intensely did at times raise my sexual energy, although certainly not to the level I heard was possible with Tantra yoga. Several times at the ashram I witnessed male disciples ask Gurudev for advice on how to control this energy. This may have been a contributing factor to my guru's lapse.

Raised within a long lineage of respected gurus in India, Gurudev had reached the pinnacle of his life's work of bringing the spiritual teachings of yoga to the West. For his services to yoga and humanity he had received honours from both the East and West. His actions were so reckless, desperately sad, and tragic, especially for his wife and nearly adult children.

In his letter, Gurudev spoke of his misgivings surrounding the role of the guru. He wrote of feeling humbled but at the same time relieved to finally be freed from the expectation that as a guru he was beyond human error. In his view the proper relationship between guru and disciple should be one of co-travellers on the path to spiritual enlightenment. He was truly sorry for the pain and disappointment his actions had caused his disciples.

Many of the disciples were understandably angry with Gurudev, especially those who had taken up residence at the ashram for many years. He had betrayed them at so many levels. Stories circulated of much crying and smashing of his photograph kept by the disciples on the altars in their rooms.

My anger with Gurudev eventually morphed into a profound sadness, almost verging on compassion. I was very sad when he fell from grace—for his sake, for mine, and for the other disciples. While his influence on me was tremendous, I hadn't invested my entire life in what he did or didn't do. I never loved him as intensely as the Hindu sacred texts say a disciple should love the guru. I didn't see him as my mother, my father, my brother, my all, my god of Gods. For me he was a spiritually enlightened soul who offered instruction and support in my quest for that Something-Other-Than. Ironically, it appears that was the sort of relationship Gurudev wanted with his disciples all along.

Instead of raging against his moral lapses, I focused on the unique experiences I'd enjoyed as Gurudev's disciple. He was a flawed man, but the messages he voiced from the Hindu sacred texts pierced my being to the core. During my time as his disciple, a profound shift in my psyche brought me an inner strength and ability to discern the essence of a matter before me. My Aunt Evelyn, who had been close to me since my childhood, observed I had changed since undertaking yoga. She couldn't say exactly how, but in her view, something about me was different. In one way at least she was correct. While I hadn't attained the peak state of enlightenment, I felt more confident walking the razor's edge of spiritual truth. For that I was, and continue to be, very grateful.

After Gurudev's fall from grace, the Kripalu yoga community in Toronto dissolved, its spiritual heart now vacated. Satsangs with my fellow yoga practitioners became fewer and fewer. With the lack of a reason to gather and share, I lost contact with the community of seekers I had enjoyed so much. Within a couple of years, my yoga teacher, Isobel/Kaveri, died of cancer. I moved the Gita with its bright orange binding, along with the Upanishads, from the top shelves of my bookcase to the bottom ones. It was the conclusion of a critical phase in my quest.

It has been twenty-five years since Gurudev left the Kripalu Yoga Center. He has atoned with the women involved in the scandal of his making and in the early 2000s established with his adult children the Amrit Yoga Institute in Florida, which serves the public as an accredited yoga school supporting an international community of professional yoga and meditation instructors. Gurudev offers a program on Shaktipat, where he passes this divine energy on to the participants in the program for healing and enlightenment. He is now in his late eighties and still actively engaged in bringing the sacred teachings of yoga to a North American audience. At times I consider visiting him at his Florida ashram before he or I depart this life. So far, I have not done so.

FOUR:

THE WAY OF POETRY

FOUR:
THE WAY OF POETRY

T he most profound and enduring outcome of my years as a disciple of Gurudev was my sudden ability not only to understand poetry but, amazingly, to be moved to write it. I became obsessed with reading the great poets, whose works revealed feelings, ideas, and potentials I had never recognized before. When I got around to trying my hand at writing my own poems, what came out were lines speaking in a voice I didn't recognize as my own. Thrilled at this glimpse of a previously unknown part of me, I took any opportunity I could to talk to people about this magnificent phenomenon called poetry. It was as though I had "gotten religion" and couldn't wait to share my experience to prevent others from missing out on what I came to call Something-Other-Than.

Many people write and read poetry. There's nothing unique about such an activity. But in my case, I considered my poems bordered on the miraculous by virtue of the suddenness of their appearance and their extreme disconnect from my previous habits and abilities. Up to this point, I had very little familiarity with poetry. I must have read a poem or two in public school. The only one I recall is the classic by Joyce Kilmer, titled "Trees," which opens with the lines, "I think that I will never see/A poem lovely as a tree" and concludes, "Poems are made by fools like me/But only God can make a tree."

No teacher in public school ever encouraged me to write poetry. Perhaps with good reason. In Grade 9, I wrote a five-stanza poem titled "What Is a Hillbilly?" It was a rant against country and western music sung by what I described in the poem as "A race of people who somehow persist/In bending our ears with such horrible sounds/That we flee from our radios with leaps and in bounds." I also inserted a line about their strumming guitars sounding "more like a rat/Caught in the claws of a nasty old cat." I submitted the poem to my high school yearbook. The day after its publication, the telephone rang at my home, and a male voice at the end of the line growled at me, "Here's some *really* great music for you to hear." The male caller went on to play a twangy country song over the telephone. I hung up the receiver, pleased and amazed at how a small poem like that could arouse such a strong reaction from a stranger. This was power of a different order: the power of words heightened by expression within the form of poetry.

In my second year of university, I signed up for a course on Romantic Poetry. Within two weeks I knew this course wasn't for me. I was dismayed to discover I couldn't understand the great poets like Lord Byron, Samuel Taylor Coleridge, William Blake, John Keats, or William Wordsworth. The truncated lines, the archaic vocabulary, and the contorted sentence structures formed a dense barrier between me and their famous poems. Not only was I put off by the vocabulary and grammar of the writing, but I was also confused by the subjects written about. At the age of seventeen, I didn't have a clue about the subtleties of the human imagination, desires, and spiritual yearnings that so engaged the poets. Within three weeks I had dropped out of the poetry course and switched to one on the economic history of the Middle East. It was obvious to me that I was not one of the chosen people destined to write poems that would endure. The structure and baffling syntax of poetry exiled me from the wisdom hidden within the lines.

By the time I met Gurudev, I was an avid reader of fiction and prose but had long given up on poetry. I still harboured an ambition to become a fiction writer but never had a clear idea how to begin. When I graduated from McGill University In the early 1960s, university courses in creative writing were scarce. More to the point, at that early age, what did I have to write about? I had the ability to manipulate words, but for what purpose? I had little worldly experience. Up to my university years, I had lived with my parents in a two-bedroom apartment in a Montreal suburb, played centre position in a local basketball league, and had won a few blue, red, and green ribbons in track and field events. The high school I attended in the late 1950s was well behaved, with no drugs, bullying, or sex clubs. Unlike Ernest Hemingway or F. Scott Fitzgerald, I had not hung out in Paris bistros or Spanish bullrings, and I had no World War II experience storming the beaches of Normandy. I couldn't even look to my personal life as a reading attraction. Fortunately, divorce and abuse—both physical and emotional—hadn't plundered my world. Growing up, I was surrounded by people who loved me, or at least wished me well in life. I read that the French novelist and essayist, Henry de Montherlant, coined the maxim "Happiness writes white," suggesting that happiness can't be described and simply won't show up on the page. The American poet Edward Hirsch debunked this common prejudice in three lines of his poem of the same name: "I don't believe that only sorrow/and misery can be written./Happiness, too, can be precise."

I hadn't yet learned that I could compensate for my limited worldly experience by reading widely, observing life about me, and above all, using my imagination. I didn't have to write only about what "really happened." I regret it took me so long to make that connection. I could have entered the writing arena much sooner instead of waiting years for the Grand Moment which would hand me the material to write about.

After university I chose to become a professional librarian, another example on my part of magical thinking. If I spent my days organizing, reading, and recommending books to clients, so my thinking went, I would absorb the necessary writing skills through a process of osmosis triggered by touching and talking about books. While I waited for my fiction writing skills to develop in this uncertain fashion, I insinuated myself into roles at work where technical writing was a requirement. For many years I wrote thick user manuals published in ringed binders that instructed library staff on the use of digital databases and computer systems for cataloguing book collections. My constant striving to be clear and succinct was superb training for a writer but limited in choice of vocabulary, character development, and plot. It would require encountering a guru in the woods and farmlands of Pennsylvania to help me break out of this limited writing genre.

Several times I was tempted to quit my information job and commit to the career of a full-time fiction writer. Yet it seemed whenever I was on the verge of taking the leap, some financial demand at home would reinforce the need for me to stay put and earn a living wage. It was clear a writer's life brought with it the spectre of poverty writ large. I should keep my day job. Hitting the bestseller list and being offered a movie contract ranked up there with winning the Irish sweepstakes. The writing dream had to remain on hold until better economic times.

For fifteen years I endured the frustration of wanting but not being able to realize my ambition to be a fiction writer. Then, at the age of thirty-five, I encountered Gurudev, and everything changed. After several months' exposure to the guru's energy field and the chanting and meditation disciplines of Kripalu yoga, I felt the urge to read poetry. Unlike the indecipherable texts of my university English course years earlier, poetry now fired up my imagination and spurred my creativity.

Although admired and revered to a high degree by a small segment of our North American culture, most people don't read or write poetry on a regular basis, even though its pedigree goes back four thousand years to the earliest form of the written word. The original poets were priests, philosophers, sovereigns, and seers who recited their poems to large crowds for their delight and inspiration, telling stirring epics of heroic warriors, myths, and stories of gods and goddesses. As keepers of their culture's oral history, these early poets held an exalted status with the people of the ancient kingdoms. Today, poetry only rises to a similar level of popularity when embedded in a song by Bob Dylan, Leonard Cohen, or Gordon Lightfoot.

The first poet who opened me up to the power of poetry was Emily Dickinson, considered one of America's greatest and most original poets. Known for breaking the stylistic mold of poetry in the nineteenth century, she peppered her lines of poetry with dashes and capitalized nouns. Beyond the uniqueness of her grammar, the way she arranged the nouns and verbs in her poems showed off her genius. Her words penetrated my imagination like a bolt of lightning, especially in the opening two verses of a poem about a mental breakdown. (Note: All her poems are untitled.)

> I felt a Funeral, in my Brain,
> And Mourners to and fro
> Kept treading–treading–till it seemed
> That Sense was breaking through–

> And when they all were seated,
> A Service, like a Drum-
> Kept beating–beating–til I thought
> My Mind was going numb– [15]

Twenty years later this poem still sends a tingling sensation up my spine and over the crown of my head. And many of her other poems have that effect on me. Initially, I wondered what this physical twinge signified. Was it an oddity of my nervous system? Later, my question was answered when I read Dickinson's response to a reviewer who had asked her how she recognized a true poem. Her reply reassured me that my physical reaction was not unique. I was in good company:

> If I read a book and it makes my whole body so cold no fire can ever warm me, I know that is poetry. If I feel physically as if the top of my head were taken off, I know that is poetry. These are the only ways I know it. Is there any other way?[16]

Dickinson was brilliant at creating and naming a state of mind or heart that I had previously not known existed. In one of her poems, I found a description of my experience at the age of three when a sweet pain welled up in my chest at the sight of a ray of sunlight streaming through a window onto the dining room table. In the first two verses of that poem, she connects the slant of light with my memorable sweet pain and gives that sensation a name:

---

15. Emily Dickinson, *Acts of Light: Poems by Emily Dickinson*, Appreciation by Jane Langton (Boston, New York: Graphic Society, 1980), 91.

16. Emily Dickinson, letter to Thomas Wentworth Higgins (1870) in *Letters of Emily Dickinson*, ed. Mabel Loomis Todd (North Chelmsford, Massachusetts: Courier Corporation, 2003).

There's a certain Slant of light,
Winter afternoons—
That oppresses, like the Heft
Of Cathedral Tunes—

Heavenly Hurt, it gives us—
We can find no scar,
But internal difference,
Where the Meanings, are—

Heavenly Hurt—Dickinson had put a name to my sweet pain. Later in the poem she equates this hurt with the "seal of Despair" caused by "the look of Death." How strange that at such a young age I could feel despair at the prospect of death, that I even understood what death meant. Yet the phrase made sense to me at a deeper level which the poet William Wordsworth so vividly described in his poem "Ode: On Intimations of Immortality from Recollections of Early Childhood." In the poem he envisions the child only recently born into life coming from afar "...trailing clouds of glory do we come/From God, who is our home": carrying within its soul the memory of a spiritual home. Life and death encountered so close together might well generate such a sweet pain, even in the soul of a child.

———

Shortly after discovering the intense, jewel-like poetry of Emily Dickinson, I came across a collection of shout-out poems called Leaves of Grass by the nineteenth-century American poet Walt Whitman. This collection rocked the poetry of its day and continues to engage readers in these modern times. Like Dickinson, Whitman broke the boundaries of centuries of poetic tradition with a unique structure and rhythmic beat to his poems. He referred to them as his "barbaric yawp over the roofs of the world."

On first reading his poems, the words bounce off the page suffused with a barbaric energy that stuns and inspires.

A major poem in this collection is called "Song of Myself," written with the same seriousness of intent as Moses' Ten Commandments. Whitman believed in the self as a spiritual entity that reflects an individual's intellectual, spiritual, and artistic being. He respected the idea that the self and the soul will eventually enjoy a mystical reunion with God. Life was a journey to uncover the identity of one's true self. Whitman left me convinced of the worth of myself irrespective of what dramatic events had happened in my life. Just being alive and human was enough to warrant me the right to be a writer.

"Song of Myself" opens with these famous, unforgettable words:

> I celebrate myself, and sing myself,
> And what I assume you shall assume,
> For every atom belonging to me as good belongs to you.[17]

Whitman was very much a man who celebrated the visible splendours of the body and nature. He didn't think one had to seek out Something-Other-Than; God existed here and now in nature and within all humans. Here is how he expressed this point of view:

> I have said that the soul is not more than the body,
> And I have said that the body is not more than the soul,
> And nothing, not God, is greater to one than one's self is,
>
> And I say to any man or woman, let your soul stand cool and
> composed before a million universes.[18]

---

17. Walt Whitman, *Leaves of Grass*, the First (1855) edition, ed. with an introduction by Malcolm Cowley (London: Penguin Books, 1976), 25.
18. Whitman, *Leaves of Grass*, https://poets.org/poem/song-myself-48.

Whitman held very controversial views on the relationship between God and humankind, views that caused his poetry to be banned in certain places. In the contest between the power of God and of Man, he comes down firmly on the side of humankind:

> I believe in the flesh and the appetites,
> Seeing hearing and feeling are miracles, and each
>   part and tag of me is a miracle.
>
> Divine I am inside and out, and I make holy what-
>   ever I touch or am touched from;
> The scent of these arm-pits is aroma finer than prayer,
> This head is more than churches or bibles or creeds.[19]

Whitman's concept of the soul and the psyche was all inclusive. He believed we have the potential within us to become many, many things. One of his more well-known lines expresses this inclusivity in a few simple, yet powerful words:

> Do I contradict myself?
> Very well then I contradict myself,
> (I am large, I contain multitudes.)[20]

The more I read poetry, the more I felt the urge to write my own poems. I spent five years immersed in learning the craft of writing poetry, engaging in critique groups and performing at public readings in coffee houses, church basements, and libraries. Nothing generated a greater thrill for me than to write a

---

19. Whitman, *Leaves of Grass*, 49.
20. Whitman, *Leaves of Grass*, 85.

poem that held together and revealed something I hadn't known previously about myself or about an idea. At such times, an inner presence seemed to be expanding and helping me move forward in understanding what that Something-Other-Than might look like or feel like.

My earliest poems focused on how Gurudev had impacted my being. I struggled with these first attempts at expressing strong feelings for which I had no easy name. While the results tended towards the melodramatic, at the time they represented my intense and sincere admiration of Gurudev.

Love of Palest Form

He encircles me with arms of simple strength
  and rocks me in the sweet embrace of an
  abundant heart.
We cling enchanted to the face of life,
  our bodies breathing in all essences of now
  and yesterday.
The pulse of life assails our ears,
  Creation chants in throbbing beats,
Investing the air with crystal sparks which fall
  as emerald dew upon the fingertips of forest giants,
Draped in flowing needled gowns of forever green.

Not enough, I cry, this love of palest form,
  To endure a life of time even though with end,
Pity you who seek here a place of nurturing warmth,
  Yet pity more the one in me, who seeks the
  love in you.[21]

---

21. Linda Cassidy, 1980 [unpublished].

I soon realized that writing a true poem was not an easy feat. One needed to do more than broadcast one's personal angst in free form, filled with sighs and groans of despair. To capture emotion with any degree of truthfulness requires a strong grasp of the craft and the discipline to show up at the writing desk on a regular basis. Yet all the craft in the world comes to nothing if not partnered with the unconscious that harbours the images and knowledge of that Something-Other-Than. The poet's muse isn't something that can be called forth at will. It's a magical gift that comes and goes as it pleases. My years of reading poetry have taught me to seek out those poets touched by the holy fire of the spirit. Sometimes, in desperation, poets will try to entice their muse to appear with liberal doses of alcohol or drugs. But that's the devil's bargain, one that can destroy body and soul.

The dream world can offer a safer and more reliable way to call up the muse and render a true poem. One morning, I awoke with a phrase flashing across my conscious mind—"the birth of my respectful and savage girl." *What an odd duality*, I thought at the time. *Respectful* and *savage*—how could such opposites exist side by side in one person? I rushed to my desk, scribbled down the phrase, and after breakfast, still under the influence of my twilight dream state, I wove a poem around the phrase:

Winter Bloom

the birth of my respectful
and savage girl
happened in the winter
deep underground
below the frostline

now it's the middle of May
and she dances solo
on a thin strong stem

swaying in a turbulence
spurred on by a keen north wind

my passion girl
my red-fleshed tulip bloom
bring me your fierce beatitude
played out in the certain knowledge
of your diminishing days.[22]

The fierceness, sensuality, and beauty of this image told me something "deep underground/below the frostline" within my psyche had emerged in an inner dance with my soul. The muse had worked while I slept and left a gift for me on awakening.

On another occasion, a painting by the Spanish Mexican surrealist painter Remedios Varo inspired my muse to pay me a visit. Varo often paints women held captive in confined spaces by forces unknown. One of her paintings, titled *Born Again*, depicts a partially naked woman bursting through the red walls of a small room and staring into a chalice of water on a table. A crescent moon floats on the surface of the water, a reflection of the real moon visible through a gaping hole in the ceiling. Within hours of viewing this painting, I had written a poem containing explosive images from my daily life:

Sacred Space

she's frantic
        to tear down
        to explode through
        to punctuate
the blandness of this space

---

22. Linda Cassidy, *Inland Waterways*, 76.

eyes wide, a crazy woman
she mourns the missing part
of the crescent moon
she thinks the holy grail
can be found in Aisle 4

in the health food section
with supplements, wheat-free bread
fatless, sugarless ingredients
alchemical potions for a transformative
diet, the guarantor of a deathless life

she's naked
she's ecstatic
she's heading across the parking lot
three plastic bags hanging from each fist
enough food for two days

she envisions
the moon's double
bobbing
on the simmering surface
of the evening's soup.[23]

Reading my poems before a live audience was a daring feat for me. Initially, I held my poems close to my vest, feeling they were private, and afraid to expose them to unfriendly fire. Gradually, I started taking chances and read them aloud, at first to small groups and eventually to larger public gatherings in community centres and restaurants willing to turn over space to struggling poets. I could tell how successful a poem was by the moments of silence at the end of the reading and before

---

23. Cassidy, *Inland Waterways*, 61.

the applause. The longer the silence, the deeper the sense of spirit in the room, the better the poem. In my mind, finding that point of quiet introspection in our noisy world is always a miracle. Audience reaction, whether favourable or dutifully polite, helped me to better gauge if my poem had reached the inner sensibilities of those listening.

———————

The inspiration for a poem often comes from the convergence of internal, unconscious cues and physical objects in the external world. Throughout my life I've been entranced by houses— photographs of houses, verbal descriptions of houses, and tours of houses. In his book *The Poetics of Space,* Gaston Bachelard, a French scientist-philosopher and student of the poetic imagination, wrote of our unconscious as being "well and happily housed" in rooms or landscapes where we have lived for a time. These real places become embodied in our dreams and imbued with meanings particular to our inner world. These landscapes designate our corner of the world from where we view new events. Whenever I read a passage in a novel describing an English country home, I always envision an historical house I lived in as a child.[24]

One landscape has insinuated itself into my dreams and unconscious thoughts over a lifetime. Not surprisingly, this is a landscape of my childhood. At the age of five, I lived on Ward's Island, one of three islands in Toronto Harbour, created almost two centuries ago from sandbars pushed around by storm waves. Large portions of the islands are filled with shallow lagoons rimmed by magnificent weeping willows trailing their feathery

---

24. Gaston Bachelard, *The Poetics of Space* (Boston: Beacon Press, 1969), 3–37.

leaves over the dark waters, where swans with curvaceous white necks glide in stately fashion.

I lived for a year with my parents and grandmother in this fairy land of water enhanced by an amusement park with a merry-go-round, an enclosure for riding ponies, and circus music blaring over speakers mounted on steel poles. No cars, only wide sidewalks and wooden boardwalks running beside sandy beaches. When it rained on Ward's Island, the children were free to run through the puddles in bare feet without fear of cars.

To reach the lagoons and our humble island house on Ward's Island, we took a ferry from the docks at Toronto Harbour. The clanging of the boarding plank, the stampede of feet rushing on board to get a seat at the front of the boat, the departing blast of the boat's horn—this cacophony of sound was part of the ritual of entering this island paradise.

But it was the lagoons with their dark and dangerous waters and the willow trees that most linger in my memory. My mother warned me many times: "Linda, don't go near the lagoon or you'll fall in the water and drown." One day I dared to do the forbidden.

I walk to the lagoon's edge, look down the length of the shaky wooden pier jutting out over the water, and take my first steps. I hesitate as the pier heaves up and down and I struggle to keep my footing. When I get to the end of the pier, I stand looking into the water that is so dark I can't see the bottom of the lagoon. In my mind I feel guilty for disobeying my mother's warnings. Somehow, I deserve to fall into the water, so I jump in. Luckily, somebody sees me struggling and pulls me up onto the pier. I walk home with water squishing through my shoes, and my braids hanging soddenly on my shoulders. Despite the guilt at taking such a rash action, I feel empowered by what I've done.

Years later, during a meditation session at the ashram, my inner self conjures up an image of the same island-scape. Once again, I sit under a willow tree on the banks of the lagoon, the summer breeze moving over the water, and the white swans paddling by in their full elegance. But my unconscious adds a dramatic detail. In my hands I hold a three-headed blood-red tulip. The specificity of this image set in a childhood landscape still puzzles and intrigues me.

Throughout my life I've always lived beside lakes, rivers, and oceans. Islands are my preferred places to live and work. For a short time I lived on the Canadian prairies in Winnipeg, Manitoba, not far from the Red River, which flooded in the spring but turned tame in the summer, fall, and winter. I missed the contrast of a large body of water next to a land mass, so I hastened back to live on the shores of Lake Ontario once again. I think of my inner psychic landscape as being one of water and islands from which arise many of my dream and creative images.

Houses, as well as landscapes, can inhabit the imaginative inner space in our psyches for a lifetime and shelter many memories and secrets of our lives, both inner and outer, which can find their way into our poems. One of the most popular evocations of a house appears in the book *Rebecca* by the mystery writer Daphne du Maurier. The book opens with the words "Last night I dreamt I went to Manderley again." Then follows a dreamlike, nostalgic description of a country home in Cornwall, England, named Manderley, which provides the psychological underpinning for this gothic story of the haunting of a woman by her husband's former wife.

My "Manderley" house was in the upscale Annex area of Toronto on Bernard Ave. I lived there when I was eight with my parents, my grandmother, and Uncle Roger, my mother's much younger brother. The three-storey house stood on a corner lot with a castle-like turret and tall windows sporting coloured glass in the top halves. Rows of tall trees top-heavy with masses of maple leaves lined each side of the street. The leaves grew so profusely they formed a tunnel of greenery that created the impression of walking through an urban forest.

Inside the foyer, the impression was of shadow and darkness, attributable to the oak panels lining the main stairwell and a pair of sliding wooden doors that led into a grand living room with high ceilings. A majestic, curving staircase led to the upstairs bedrooms, while a narrow back staircase led from the kitchen quarters to the servants' rooms.

The Bernard Avenue house was primarily a residence for blinded war veterans of World War II. The second-floor rooms were reserved for men being trained at the CNIB (Canadian National Institute for the Blind) office across the street. For the most part, the blind men came and went during the day, having little contact with me or my grandmother. I shared a room on the second floor with my parents. During the day, I helped my grandmother clean the rooms. We used the staircase meant originally for the servants. The blind men didn't take their meals in the house but dined at the CNIB offices across the street. I did, however, make a connection with one boarder. His name was Jimmy. His eyes always stared straight ahead, rarely blinking, and he walked with a white cane. In my memory, Jimmy sits in a chair with a book in his lap. He reads to me the story of Little Red Riding Hood. "Jimmy," I say, shaking with excitement, "you can see! You can see!" He smiles and says nothing. But I know I have witnessed a miracle.

I associated the rooms upstairs with darkness and all things scary. At night I would tiptoe past my sleeping parents, open the door slowly, and head down the long, partially lit corridor to the bathroom. The cold linoleum floor on my bare feet made me shiver. The bathroom was large with a voluminous bathtub supported by fat ceramic feet. The toilet reached the height of a queen's throne, making mounting and dismounting the seat a great effort for a child. I would tiptoe back to my parents' room, observing a light under Uncle Roger's bedroom door. I could detect the whiff of cigarette smoke, and jazz music played softly on his radio. The rooms occupied by the blind men were at the far end of the hall. I never saw lights under their doors. I guess their eyes could make no use of light.

One night I was awakened by the acrid smell of smoke. My father grabbed me by the hand, and we rushed downstairs out into the backyard. Firemen arrived minutes later. We huddled anxiously with our neighbours, watching the firemen disappear into the house. Finally, they dragged a burning mattress out of the side door. "Somebody was smoking," growled one of the men as they threw the mattress to the ground. "Probably one of the blind guys." I wasn't at all sure that was the case. Maybe it was Uncle Roger who had dropped a burning cigarette butt on the mattress. But I said nothing. I adored my uncle as I would an older brother and I didn't want to get him into trouble.

During these years spent in a boarding house for blind men, I frequently played a game with my friends called "blind man's buff." One player, who is "It," wears a handkerchief over his eyes and is spun around several times until disoriented. The other players, who are not blindfolded, scatter so as not to be caught by the blind man. If they are caught or touched by him, they must put the blindfold on themselves. Originally an adult game, the blind man was often struck or buffeted, providing the name "blind man's buff" to the game in the old English meaning of buff—a small push. Playing this game, I learned at a physical level what it would be like to have no vision and attempt to interact with my surroundings. It was frightening and anxiety provoking to the extreme.

Over the years, this experience of being a sightless person has appeared repeatedly in my dreams. Typically, I'm driving a car when suddenly I lose my eyesight. Even though blinded, I'm unable to stop the car and get out. Instead, I'm forced to drive on into the night, sightless and in constant fear of running off the road and crashing into a tree. Eventually I wake up in a state of terror.

When I encountered the unexpected spiritual undercurrents in poetry, I went in search of an explanation. Eventually, I found one possibility. In the yogic tradition the third eye, also called the mind's eye, is purported to be one of the energy centres, or chakras, of the body, located in the middle of the forehead slightly above the juncture of the eyebrows. The Indian spiritual tradition refers to the third eye as the gate that leads to the inner realms and spaces associated with higher consciousness. It's thought to symbolize a state of enlightenment that includes intuition, imagination, and insight. The opening of this psychic eye can happen following the practice of yogic disciplines.

In my research, I also found mention of a psychic fourth eye, which is supposed to help us see beyond our three-dimensional world and its limitations. This fourth eye relates to the ability to feel and understand the language of poetry. According to Hindu belief, the spiritual energy at the ashram might have opened this invisible eye and made me receptive to the power embedded in poetry. I have no way of knowing for certain if this is the "right" answer, but in the absence of any other explanation, it's one I'm willing to accept in accordance with Keats's recommendation to assume an attitude of "negative capability" when approaching the mystery of the unknown without necessarily insisting on fact and reason.

Gradually, I came to feel a strong connection between poetry and the spiritual domain of what I had named Something-Other-Than. In fact, philosophers and theologians have debated this connection for many years and continue to do so to this day. Since 2011, a series of international interdisciplinary conferences known as *The Power of the Word Conferences* has delved deeply into the relationship between religious prayers on the one hand and poetry on the other. The conference participants have moved closer to the notion of the poetic form of writing as being a way to enhance spiritual intelligence.

Given this acknowledged connection, I was reassured that poetry was not a distraction from my spiritual quest; rather, an enhancement and a tool to access the invisible world of spirit. Poetry could be my lifeline to reach out toward the universal mind, a signifier of my Something-Oher-Than. The poet who most strongly confirmed this viewpoint for me was the German-language poet and novelist Rainer Maria Rilke, widely acknowledged as being among the greatest of the twentieth-century poets.

A divine, inner inspiration drove Rilke to an unheard level of quality and productivity in his poetry. In his masterpiece the *Duino Elegies,* the poems arrived perfectly on the page, with hardly a single word needing to be altered. He wrote the first of the elegies at Duino Castle in 1912, perched on a steep cliff overlooking the Adriatic Sea, near Trieste, Italy. In a letter to a friend, he described the January day as cold and sunny with a violent north wind blowing. He took a path down the cliffs to the beach, where he walked back and forth while pondering a business matter. All at once, he was stopped by an inhuman voice he took to be an angel, calling out from the raging wind and the clouds: "Who, if I cried out, would hear me among the angels' hierarchies?"

Rilke immediately took out his notebook, wrote down the sentence, and returned to the castle, where the rest of the poem poured out of him. He told his friend that he felt the voice represented a higher power that inhabited him and dictated the poem to him.

This voice from the clouds resulted in the greatest and most powerful creative output ever recorded for a poet. Rilke wrote more than two hundred poems in two weeks. The poems required no editing, and they are considered some of the most profound written over the last two centuries. Here are the first eight lines of the "dictated" elegy:

> Who, if I cried out, would hear me among the angels'
> hierarchies? And even if one of them pressed me
> suddenly against his heart: I would be consumed
> in that overwhelming existence. For beauty is nothing
> but the beginning of terror, which we still are just able to
>   endure,
> and we are so awed because it serenely disdains
> to annihilate us. Every angel is terrifying.[25]

Ten years later, in 1922, Rilke experienced another intense event in another masterpiece, The Sonnets to Orpheus. He called the event "a hurricane in the spirit," which he described as "disappearing into the god." He spent days and nights pacing back and forth in his room, "howling unbelievably vast commands and receiving signals from cosmic space and booming out to them my immense salvoes of welcome." Within three days he had finished the first part of The Sonnets to Orpheus, "the most mysterious, the most enigmatic dictation I have ever endured and achieved; the whole first part was written down in a single breathless obedience." In three weeks, he had written another thirty-eight sonnets and finished the Duino Elegies started ten years earlier. These new poems

---

25. Rainier Maria Rilke, *Duino Elegies and The Sonnets to Orpheus* (New York: Random House, 2009), 3.

were also born perfect, with no editing required. Stephen Mitchell, Rilke's literary translator, described this writing event as "the most astonishing burst of inspiration in the history of literature."26

We are left to wonder if Rilke's poems truly represent the voice of God as channelled through his part of the universal mind. Lacking any way to verify Rilke's experience (except by virtue of the amount and quality of the work he produced in such a short period of time), many followers of the traditional faiths might well consider this view of the *Elegies* and the *Sonnets of Orpheus* to be blasphemous. Moses spoke to God directly, as did Muhammad and Jesus Christ. Anyone else who claims a direct connection to the divine spirit is open to accusations of being delusional, a bit of a flake. On the other hand, some poets and scholars consider it unlikely that the story of the human soul's desire for God has ended in only two or three scriptures written thousands of years ago. They believe it much more likely that our souls' journeys will continue to evolve. Great poets like Rilke will contribute a modern voice to the ancient holy scriptures.

My poetry was published for the first time in 1984 in *IRON*, an English literary journal of some reputation. The two poems I submitted earned me the grand sum of five pounds. I cherished that small stipend more than the much larger ones I'd received for my technical writing. Those five pounds represented an acknowledgement of my poetry, and that made all the difference. I was now a published poet. *[Note: I wrote these early poems under my married name, Linda Farmer.]*

When She Was Five

She rides
his lacquered flanks,

---

26. Rilke, *Duino Elegies and The Sonnets to Orpheus*, 81.

hugs his surge and fall
between strong legs.
Her bloodlines spin
hot webs
on a bony frame.

In a room
a grass-cut breeze
ruffles white curtains
along a window ledge.
A fly hums and bumbles
against the pane.
She inhales sunbeams.

When she was five
her mother came
into the room
and said, "Katie, dear,
let your sister
have a turn now
on the rocking horse."[27]

Corn Field in Winter

Earth glares at husband sky,
Grinds her corn husk stubs
Like dry shark's teeth
Broken near the roots.

Stubble rot crackles.
Her word-winds split the rows

---

27. Farmer, *IRON Magazine*, No. 43 (Tyne & Wear, UK: IRON Press, 1984), 37.

And blow a sulphurous breath
Hard across his face.

She demands her rights.
New roots, new growth,
A summer coronet of broadband leaves,
Green ribbons for a corn silk crop.

Husband sky remains unmoved,
Hides the hot transforming rain
Behind the blind whites
Of a February eye.

The universe will turn, she says.
She'll be on top then
And spit black cinders
Into his pretty blue eyes.[28]

At the same time *IRON* published my poetry, the University of London accepted me into its juried poetry workshop. I began to entertain the hope that I was getting closer to the point where I might dare to call myself a poet.

In 2010, after two decades of working at the craft of poetry while keeping my day job, an independent press published my first collection of poems: *Inland Waterways: Poems from a Peaceable Kingdom.* The collection narrates moments in the ebb and flow of a woman's inner life as she passes through waypoints along her spiritual quest to the sea. It begins at the headwaters of a strong river, traverses a riverbed, conquers cataracts and

---

28. Farmer, *IRON Magazine*, No. 43, 36.

floodplains—finally ending at the fingers of a land mass that reaches out from an estuary into the eternal sea.

One of the poems describes how a hunger of the body can transform into a hunger for the spirit:

Steering for the Light

There are all kinds of ways
to steer through the dark
when a moonless, starless night
leaves you in a panic
unsure of your next breath
not knowing if death will smother
the starlight in you leaving
only the mediocre behind.

Sometimes pouring tea from a teapot
sipping it slowly from a white china-cup
can nourish your love of ritual
turn darkness into a religious experience.

After midnight you can witness wildlife
on large-screen TV in breathtaking,
eye-popping colour, marvel at how
a pelican can scoop frogs and salamanders
into its orange pouch for later consumption,
marvel at how naked humans can fornicate
on TV and still keep a straight face.

If nothing works and you start to weep
you can cauterize the hole in your heart
with a prayer of indulgence addressed
to the Supreme Deity of your choosing.
This too can be a religious experience.
If your prayer goes unanswered

and your heart seems not up to its task
you can steer through the darkness
prepare an insomniac's feast where you sizzle
the pan, sear the flesh, chop and dice
and slice until the vegetables fly
drizzle the chocolate on whatever's at hand
nibble, chew and taste and swallow
and suddenly you're into the light.[29]

After the publication of *Inland Waterways*, I diversified my writing to include not only poetry but also fiction. I began work on a mystery novel based on an ancient Mesopotamian myth that chronicles the journey of Inanna (Queen of Heaven) and her descent to the underworld to visit her recently widowed sister, Ereshkigal, Queen of the Dead. Publishing a novel had been my original goal before I was hijacked by my yoga-induced passion for poetry. I reimagined the Sumerian myth as a modern murder mystery involving two long-estranged sisters who are brought together in a face-off sparked by the murder of a drug lord and the kidnapping of the son of one of the sisters.

I self-published the novel in March 2020, ten years after my poetry collection. I titled it *The Long Revenge*. Unfortunately, the same month my novel hit the marketplace, a viral pandemic swept the world, creating panic, destitution, existential dread, and death wherever it gained a foothold. Human gatherings of all kinds were severely restricted, including book launches and literary readings. Schools were closed and people were mandated by governments to wear masks. Illness had arrived on a universal scale not seen since the flu epidemic of 1918. Suddenly, humanity was facing the spectre of death as an everyday presence poised for the right moment to attack. Consequently, *The*

---

29. Cassidy, *Inland Waterways*, 67.

Long Revenge did not receive its moment in the sun. I intend to reissue it after the pandemic has passed.

I can't precisely quantify how poetry contributed to my spiritual journey except to say it was critical to any success I encountered. It served as my spirit's touchstone and personal church. When I get too busy with the daily demands of life and let my poetry books languish on the shelf, a subtle melancholy insinuates itself into my being. Then I remember to read a poem, or even better, write one. Voilà! The universe sings again, and I inhabit my daily existence with a greater awareness of the people, happenings, and natural life all around me.

The miracle of coming to poetry through yoga and being a disciple of Gurudev was the defining moment of my quest. I consider the hundreds of master poets who preceded me to be my companions, my tribe, my fellow seekers. Maybe they didn't find the answer to existence, but they never gave up. They kept following the golden thread, that inner presence running through their lives and urging them toward a higher level of consciousness and truth.

In his cycle of love poems to God titled *The Book of Hours*, Rilke expresses his aspirations as a poet, which I have taken on as my credo.

> I believe in all that has never yet been spoken.
> I want to free what waits within me
> so that what no one has dared to wish for
>
> may for once spring clear
> without my contriving.
>
> If this is arrogant, God, forgive me,

but this is what I need to say.
May what I do flow from me like a river,
no forcing and no holding back,
the way it is with children.

Then in these swelling and ebbing currents,
these deepening tides moving out, returning,
I will sing you as no one ever has,

streaming through widening channels
into the open sea.[30]

Rilke certainly has laid out a high bar for poets. Still, I live in hope that one day my imagination and psyche will edge a bit closer to meeting his standard.

---

30. Rainer Maria Rilke, *Rilke's Book of Hours: Love Poems to God*, trans. Anita Barrows and Joanna Macy (New York: Riverhead Books/Penguin Group, 2005), 65.

FIVE:

IN THE DOLDRUMS

FIVE:

IN THE DOLDRUMS

n the world of sailing there exists a set of weather conditions that occurs in the equatorial region of the Atlantic Ocean. Noted for its light, unpredictable winds, interspersed with sudden storms and blazing hot air temperatures, these unfavourable conditions can last for weeks at a time. It requires immense patience and skillful sailing to break free of this weather belt. The state of being becalmed in these waters is popularly referred to as "being in the doldrums," a phrase that has come to denote both a nautical location and an emotional state of mind.

The six years from 1995 to 2001 turned out to be my spiritual doldrums. The momentum of my inner search for Something-Other-Than had dropped away, beginning with Gurudev's fall from grace and the subsequent dispersal of the spiritual community that had grown around him. No longer able to share the group energy generated by satsangs with Gurudev, chanting, and meditation, I found myself on my own once again, but with one difference: I was armed with a knowledge of spiritual practices learned during my years as a disciple, one which unfortunately I did not take full advantage of. Looking back, I can see that I, as well as many other disciples, relied too much on our guru's unique inner powers to provide the motivational jet fuel to stay with our independent practices. Instead of building my own tower of spiritual strength through the practices, I let myself ride on the coattails of Gurudev's abilities. I had become lazy and complacent in my practice of yoga.

My spiritual quest had now entered a phase of freefall. I no longer possessed the spiritual shield of a guru and his inspired teachings to keep bad things from happening to me and the ones I loved. My encounters with Gurudev made me feel safe, secure, and untouchable by the nasty, painful events that cropped up in everyone else's life. Magical thinking once again.

In fact, several storm clouds had already begun to gather on the horizon, beginning with my father's sudden death in 1979 at sixty-seven, four years after I met Gurudev. I described the circumstances of his death in a poem with these lines: *He left us last year/Not yet old, more than young/Exploding across the black parquet/Telephone in his hand/And his heart in shreds.* While Dad's passing was a shock, the collateral damage done to my mother caused me far more angst. Anxiety and depression became a permanent feature of her character that smothered our interactions. Being her only child, I was her chief emotional support, a service I found difficult to provide amongst the demands of my own family and career. It was a problem with no solution at hand.

Three years later, in 1982, my husband's work required we move to Peaslake, a small village in Surrey, England. Here we lived a fairy tale existence in a tiny house called Anchusa Cottage, built on the edge of a vast forest. It wouldn't have surprised me to have met Little Red Riding Hood running through the trees with the Big Bad Wolf in hot pursuit. During the weekdays, my sons attended a nearby boarding school as day students, and my husband travelled to Denmark for his work, leaving me free to pursue my spiritual quest in any way I chose.

Lacking any direct contact with Gurudev or my yoga community in Toronto, it was difficult in faraway Peaslake to keep the link to Kripalu yoga alive. For a time, I edited transcripts of Gurudev's lectures sent me by the ashram. That helped a lot, but it wasn't enough. I sought out yoga classes, but they didn't exist in the remote country villages of Surrey. It was at this point I decided to focus on poetry for my spiritual practice. My passion for this art form had sprung from my contact with Gurudev. It made sense to lean on poetry as the way to stay connected.

I spent the morning hours at my writing desk and after lunch roamed the surrounding woods, walking for miles without seeing a soul. The trees stood straight and tall, giving the majestic impression of a cathedral. The village women told me they wouldn't walk in the woods alone; it was too dangerous. The prospect never crossed my mind.

I attended a poetry course at the University of London and participated in writing retreats led by well-known British poets in a thatched eleventh-century manor house in Totleigh Barton, Devon. There I found a tribe of poets who took poetry as seriously or more so than I did. My efforts in sharpening up my craft paid off when a well-regarded English literary journal published three of my poems and, to my extreme delight, paid me a few pounds to publish them. I framed the cheque. I could now consider myself a paid poet.

My life was not devoted exclusively to poetry. In the weekday afternoons, I whizzed around the country lanes of rural Surrey by car, taking in scenes of cows and horses huddled picturesquely under trees in green pastures while adjusting to driving on the wrong side of the road and using a standard gear shift. I lunched at vintage English pubs, where I ordered the traditional ploughman's lunch—cheese, pickled onions, and crusty bread washed down with a superb apple cider. I often popped into London by train to attend poetry readings featuring major British poets. At the end of the day, I would pick up my sons (now twelve and thirteen) from school and we would spend the evenings together.

On the weekends, we travelled as a family, absorbing British country life and visiting the architectural gems in London. We headed off for longer trips, exploring Paris and the Loire Valley of France. On one two-week excursion, we sailed the Aegean Sea around the Mediterranean island of Corfu. An exciting trip, although it pushed me beyond my sailing comfort zone. Fortunately, my two sons had acquired a few nautical skills during the trip and could help their father. Two images, or should I say omens, from that voyage remain transfixed in my mind: the first image was the body of a young puppy floating beside the bow of our boat, having fallen into the water and drowned; the second instance occurred on a beach where a group of young men held another young man upside down by the feet as he flopped lifelessly in the air—he had drowned. Shortly after this, Fraser's back condition flared up and I had to take over more of the hands-on sailing. I was petrified much of the time, trying to look competent for the sake of our sons.

We returned to Toronto in 1985. By then poetry had overtaken yoga as my spiritual practice. I stayed with poetry as it came the closest to opening myself to an experience of Something-Other-Than. To improve my skills, I took a poetry course at York University with the well-known Canadian poet bpNichol, whom one critic called the Walt Whitman of Canada. An internationally acclaimed avant-garde poet, bpNichol wrote what was called concrete poetry, where the words are arranged on the page into patterns that strive to reveal a meaning beyond what the words can do on their own. His work spanned the boundaries of poetry to include visual art, sound, and prose. Generous in his critiques of his students' work, he always found something positive to say about every poem brought into class, no matter how poorly executed. I asked him once how he was able to recognize the positive in our efforts. He replied with a modest smile: "My poetry is so unconventional; I can always find something to admire in every poem I read." He was right about his poetry. I tried to get into it but wasn't successful. Yet the manner in which bpNichol turned his experimental poetry into support for up-and-coming poets, no matter their style, I found admirable. I noticed he brought a cushion to class, saying it was to support his back. A few months later, he died from an operation on his back at the insanely young age of forty-three. I still keenly remember his kindness and I regret I couldn't decipher the imaginative key to his work. Most likely my shortcoming rather than his.

Making a living as a poet was looking like a dicey proposition with uncertain prospects and low, low remuneration. My family circumstances—a husband initiating a second career as an engineering consultant and two sons about to enter high school with university not far behind—required an all-hands-on-deck approach to maintaining a stable revenue stream to ensure financial stability. This was not the time to give up my day job for the life of a poet. So I became a technical writer, a suitable compromise, as it kept me involved as a writer, fiddling with words and striving for clarity of expression. While I enjoyed the job—it was, after all, a form of writing—I found the vocabulary of technical writing limited, with little to stir the imagination and fire up the unconscious. I sharpened my vocabulary skills by reading my poems to modest audiences in cafés and libraries, where I met a supportive network of fellow poets. These contacts reminded me that writing poetry is a sane, miraculous thing to do, possessing purpose and value and enjoyed by many people.

In the mid-1980s, my husband and I purchased a blue-hulled sailboat we named *Blue Heron*. Our sons, Mark and Peter, became avid, skillful sailors, participating in club match races and taking the helm in cruises from one end of Lake Ontario to the other. As the fictional family narrative goes, involvement in sailing kept our boys out of bars, off drugs, and out of pool halls. I was able to take the helm of the boat (steer it) in calm conditions, throw lines (ropes) onto the dock, and pull protective fenders on and off the deck. Unfortunately, I never got the hang of anticipating the interplay of wind and sails. Trimming the sails in accordance with wind conditions is a core sailing skill I failed to acquire. But I did serve up tasty meals in the cockpit and always made sure the Chardonnay wines were well chilled.

The late 1980s were a mixture of good and not-so-good times. The best, most sustaining feature was my family life. Living with my husband and two sons brought me such emotional riches, I often wondered why I was seeking Something-Other-Than when I had it right here, now, today, in our home. Holding your newborn baby in your arms for the first time is a life-altering spiritual encounter. The love streams out with an intensity unmatched by anything else. And sharing a home and life with a kind, intelligent man is right at the top of my list of desirable supports for a spiritual quest.

The not-so-good part of the late 1980s was my mother's continuing state of depression and anxiety over my father's death six years earlier. Our relationship became more strained. I almost drowned in waves of guilt at not being able to provide her the kind of emotional solace she needed so badly. It was the worst of all problems, an existential issue with no practical solution except to endure.

I kept on with my career and watched Mark and Peter grow into manhood and prepare themselves for their own lives. Yoga had faded for me, and while I still clung to poetry as my spiritual practice, I needed a stronger wind to fill my sails and move me forward. All I could see in my mind's eye was smooth, glassy water where I suspected even the fish were bored. Then, as the decade turned to the 1990s, an event blindsided me and shook me to the core. I was diagnosed with breast cancer. I was only forty-nine, and contrary to my deeply held belief that I was immortal, I realized no exception would be made in my case. I was going to die sometime soon. Here it was—the Void—the reason our species spends so much time and energy seeking the meaning of the universe and our role in the cosmic spectacle.

Luckily, the cancer was detected early and was treatable. Still, I needed to undergo minor surgery, endure weeks of radiation, and swallow torpedo-shaped yellow pills for five years before being declared "cancer-free." Later I came to realize this medical verdict should be rendered with a qualifier, it being more accurate to say "cancer-free *for the moment*." The love of my family softened the ferocious arrival of the leader of the four Horsemen of the Apocalypse—the Pale Rider, the spectre of death.

Yoga and the Hindu wisdom I'd absorbed in the sacred texts of the Gita and the Upanishads did not ease my panic. No matter what I had read and experienced so far on my quest, I was not prepared to deal with such an in-your-face, existential crisis. Prepared or not, I followed the medical guidelines and worked through the five years of active treatment for my cancer as I built up my information consultancy. No divine presence reassured me not to worry or be sad. The universe seemed to have no reaction to what happened to my body. I envied those folk I read about who laid their problems at God's feet and said everything will be well. But I couldn't fake such a belief. My husband, sons, and friends were my only support as far as they could travel with me. But in the core of me I was on my own—again. Just me and my cancer locked in a "danse macabre" to join my ancestors in the graveyard of future aspirations.

―――――――

By 1995 I was truly mired in a spiritual doldrum. No yoga, no meditation, no gatherings with other seekers, no chanting, not even yoga asanas. Poetry slouched around the fringes of my days, but I didn't make enough room on my daily calendar to accomplish anything of significance. Too often I told myself I was too tired, or I wasn't in the mood—two of the lamest excuses in the endless stream of excuses cited by people trying to avoid responsibility for not getting a task accomplished. The business of engaging with the demands of the everyday material world had pushed aside the nebulous world of the spirit. The yearning for that Something-Other-Than had gone deep underground.

Our family life had hit a plateau. Our two sons finished university and left home to pursue their adult lives. We were sad to see them leave, even though we knew it was a sign of our success as parents that they were ready and eager to leave. A foreign buy-out forced Fraser to take an early retirement from the natural gas corporation where he had worked for over thirty years. Building an independent consulting business was proving more difficult than he had hoped. I had set up an information consultancy, but it wasn't flourishing.

We took stock and decided to seek another adventure in our lives before our aging bodies cramped our style. It was time to push our way out of the doldrums. I was fifty-four and Fraser fifty-six—far too early to retire from the work world. We were both energetic and keen to explore more of the world. My cancer had dropped out of sight for over five years, and Fraser's health was still robust. The only fly in the ointment was that perennial affliction—a lack of money to sustain the comfortable lifestyle we had become accustomed to. The erratic nature of working as a consultant means longish stretches between paycheques and the constant anxiety of looking for the next "gig."

At that point, the stars in our universe came into alignment. I was offered a full-time position in Nova Scotia as the director of an academic library consortium, and it came with a fulsome salary. Fraser could run his consultancy from anywhere—Toronto or Halifax, it didn't make any logistical difference. My new position with its steady salary would provide the financial bridge to tie us over while Fraser grew his business. And as an extra bonus, a move to Nova Scotia allowed him to indulge his passion for blue water sailing.

The decision made, we sold our house and *Blue Heron* and drove to a new home in the fishing community of Blandford, Nova Scotia, located at the tip of the Aspotogan Peninsula. Our house stood on a cliff overlooking the ocean on thirteen acres of scrub land beaten down by the winds from the Atlantic Ocean. Despite this isolated situation, it only took fifty minutes to drive to my job in Halifax. One of the first things we did was purchase a slightly larger sailboat, which we named *Greensleeves*. The name was inspired by the green stripes painted along its white hull from stem to stern. *Greensleeves* was a beauty to look at and roomy—ideal for exploring the eastern coastline of North America.

Walking the cliff edge of our property and gazing out to sea evoked the image of a mythic landscape designed by the Nordic gods. When I mowed our acres of lawn, the seagulls would swoop down on me from the blue sky and then dart out over the ocean toward the horizon. It felt like mowing a lawn on the estate of a god. This otherworldly feeling was enhanced by a graveyard inscribed with names and dates of early settlers from the 1700s and 1800s. The thin gravestones stood slightly askew in the lumpy turf, many of them marking the graves of infants and children. Descendants of the family names on the headstones could still be found living in Blandford over two hundred years later.

Fraser and I spent four years in Blandford, living in the shadow of the wild mighty North Atlantic. The seascape was foreign to us city dwellers accustomed to sidewalks and asphalt roads. Incandescent sunsets, pounding ocean waves, and rocky seaside cliffs replaced the quiet tree-lined city streets of our youth and adult lives. Sailing the smooth waters and flat shores of Lake Ontario paled in significance to sailing *Greensleeves* along the rugged shoreline of south Nova Scotia. The rocky islands and deep bays that punctuated the shoreline made us gasp at their majestic beauty.

Although our time in Blandford was enjoyable, especially the time sailing in such natural beauty, overall, my strongest memories of the place are not the happiest ones. In my mind our seaside home became entangled in a series of sad and tragic events both personal and public. Shortly after our arrival, I received a letter from the Kripalu Yoga Fellowship announcing Yogi Desai's resignation as spiritual director and his note admitting to inappropriate sexual behaviour with female disciples. Two years later, my mother died in Toronto, as did my mother's sister, Aunt Evelyn, whom I considered to be my second mother. Months later, Uncle Roger, my mother's brother, also died. In a short period of time, my mother's entire family had departed this life, taken out like wooden pins in a bowling alley. I now found myself reluctantly occupying the lead position in the generational train chugging its way toward eternity. As for my job, it didn't fit my essentially introverted nature and my preference to perform a task rather than organize others to do it. After two years I resigned my position as Executive Director and returned to my information consultancy.

It wasn't just these personal events that marked these four years in Blandford as a dark time in my memory. Three major tragedies took place within sight of our seaside home. On September 2, 1998, Swissair Flight 111 from New York City to Geneva flew directly over our house at 10:28 p.m. and minutes later crashed into the frigid waters of St. Margaret's Bay, close to Halifax. All 229 passengers and crew died on impact. I recall the house shuddering slightly as it hit the ocean's dark surface. The next morning, I sat on a boulder by the ocean's edge, trying to come to terms with the enormity and closeness of this tragedy. I looked down at my feet and observed objects from the doomed flight floating in the waves, including a cosmetics case containing a toothbrush and a tube of toothpaste. Tufts of orange material, once a part of the insulation from the airplane, had washed up on shore. Later that day, a troop of Canadian Armed Forces marched down our driveway and climbed down the cliff to the shore looking for debris from the aircraft and possibly body parts. A rumour in the village claimed a leg had been washed up on the shoreline a mile down the coast.

Not long after the Swissair crash, a teenaged youth who lived in a house at the end of our lane shot and killed his parents. I had met the mother several times. She taught kindergarten and was looking forward to an expanded program for her beloved pupils. Her husband was active in the community and coached the local soccer team. Drugs were rumoured to be a significant factor in the son's actions in this Greek tragedy. In a newspaper interview several years later the sister spoke with bitterness of how her parents had done so much for her brother and she could not forgive him for how he repaid them. Her brother was still in prison and, since the trial, she had refused to speak to him.

I attended the funeral of the parents, held in a small ocean-front church within sight of my home. A Scottish bagpipe played the mourners into the church, which couldn't accommodate all the villagers who turned out. The sister stood before the mourners, her back to the stony shoreline of the Atlantic Ocean, her hands and forearms shaking with grief and shock—at eighteen her entire family wiped out violently by her younger brother.

The third tragedy took place on Big Tancook Island, visible on the horizon from our cliff-edge property. A man who had recently returned from a tour on the oil rigs in the North Atlantic killed his two children, walked past his wife, and went outside, where he shot himself. I heard of another suicide further along the peninsula, but there were no details. It seemed living in a landscape fit for the gods did not necessarily guarantee human happiness.

In 1999, Fraser and I planned our return to Toronto. While Nova Scotia was a beautiful province, it wasn't where we wanted to spend the rest of our lives. The locals were friendly, but they always perceived those not born locally as *come-from-aways*. I didn't expect we would ever feel truly connected to the community. It surprised me to realize how hard it can be after a certain age to sink emotional roots into a new place. I missed Toronto, its skyscrapers lining the shore of Lake Ontario, the bustle and excitement of the downtown streets, the libraries and universities, the museums and art galleries. Toronto was where I was born and raised until the age of eleven, and the place I instinctively called home. And, above all, we missed our sons, who still lived in Toronto and had not, as we thought, taken off for foreign ports.

As we considered the details of our return, we realized an opportunity presented itself. There was no rush to get back to Toronto, and we had the option of sailing down the Eastern Seaboard to Florida and maybe on into the Caribbean. Instead of heading out to the stormy Atlantic Ocean, we chose to travel by way of the Intracoastal Waterway (ICW), an inland waterway composed of a series of natural inlets, saltwater rivers, bays, and canals that runs along the Eastern Seaboard of the United States. The ICW provided us with a sheltered route down the coast, which was much more in keeping with my sailing skills.

At the end of September 1999, we set sail on *Greensleeves* from Mahone Bay, Nova Scotia, crossing the Gulf of Maine to the town of Bar Harbor. In my imagination, I viewed this sea voyage as my version of the legendary Greek hero Odysseus's return voyage after his victory in the Trojan War. It was my way to get out of the spiritual doldrums and prepare myself for a return to my search for Something-Other-Than. It took Odysseus ten years to return home to his kingdom on the island of Ithaca, during which he endured a series of fantastic encounters with terrible storms and dangerous women who could turn men into swine and lure them to forget their life's mission. He even drank blood with the dead. My adventures on this sea journey were, of course, not nearly so dramatic or dangerous as those experienced during Odysseus's voyage, but they did stir up some anxious moments and assumed a mythical, poetic sensibility in my imagination.

Our sea voyage did not begin well. Due to a delay in closing the real estate deal on our house, we left our departure until September, the start of hurricane season. Wintery temperatures overtook us, causing a thin sheet of ice to coat the decks, making it perilous to move about the decks and adjust sails. The winds blowing off the Atlantic cut like razors on our cheeks. On top of this, *Greensleeves'* engine began to fail periodically, requiring us to call for assistance from the Coast Guard to get into port without catching our propellor on the lines attached to the hundreds of lobster pots spread across the mouth of each port.

The cold weather and our faulty engine forced us to haul *Greensleeves* out of the water and ship it south by truck to the warmer coastal city of Charleston, South Carolina. While *Greensleeves* lurched her way ignominiously down Interstate 95 on the back of a flatbed truck, we rented a car for two weeks, checked into hotels on the way, and ate out three times a day. This was not turning out to be the inexpensive live-aboard life-style we had planned. The extra costs blew a huge hole in our budget.

We joined up with *Greensleeves* in Charleston and continued down the ICW. It was blessedly warm all the way to Miami. We took our time sailing down the seaboard, or should I say motoring. The ICW is only a bit wider than a normal ditch leaving no room to manoeuvre a boat by sail. The engine was all-important, as there was no option to raise sails. *Greensleeves'* engine misbehaved the entire way, shutting down at the most inconvenient times, leaving us bobbing uncontrollably in the "ditch" while oncoming boats made their way carefully around us to avoid a collision.

We stopped at towns along the way, including Beaufort, St. Augustine, Savannah, and Fort Lauderdale. We sauntered down the streets of southern towns, taking in the two-storey white antebellum houses with iron gates and the gnarled oak trees draped with grey-green Spanish moss along the streets. This was my introduction to the American South; my senses throbbed with the scent of lush vegetation enhanced by tropical temperatures and sea air. In late November we arrived in the salt marshes and tidal creeks of South Carolina in the middle of the shrimping season. The seascape of the tidal creeks was like nothing I'd seen before. Wide channels of sea water snaked through broad swaths of short grasses. As we motored slowly along one of these channels toward an inland dock, we were confronted by the imposing sight of a shrimp boat making its way out to sea. Broad in the beam with outrigging seemingly as wide as that of a 747 airliner and draped with nets for dragging the sea bottom, the shrimp boats were an imposing sight. That night we anchored in the tidal creek amongst the tall grasses, being careful not to anchor in a channel used by the shrimp boats setting out at night.

In December, boaters draped the bowsprits, transoms, and shrouds of their boats with strings of Christmas lights. It was a magnificent, wondrous sight to be part of a parade of boats motoring down the ICW in a mass of multicoloured lights enhanced by the notes of traditional Christmas carols floating across the water from passing boats. The spectacle surpassed any Christmas display I had seen up north.

Three months after leaving Nova Scotia, in the last days of the millennium, we tied *Greensleeves* to the docks in Coconut Grove, South Miami. Over the next couple of weeks, after seeing to our cranky motor at a local marina, we walked the city, indulged in seafood of all varieties, and sailed farther south to Key Largo, where we drank rum cocktails and watched the sun go down in a blaze of red glory. One of my peak moments there was sitting at the desk in Ernest Hemingway's house where he had written *Green Hills of Africa* and *The Snows of Kilimanjaro*, among other renowned works. The grounds of the house were populated by forty six-toed "polydactyl" cats, most of them said to be direct descendants of the cats owned by Hemingway.

While living in the marina onboard *Greensleeves*, we discovered a fascinating and varied community of boat people. One was a man in his late fifties who lived alone with his black mongrel dog named Max. He would take his dog into the shower room at the marina, where my husband overheard him talking to Max like he was his soul mate, which he probably was for lack of a human one. My husband was greatly moved by this animal-human interchange.

I spoke with a woman in her early sixties who lived alone on her sailboat between her annual solo ocean crossings between the Atlantic and the Mediterranean. Her sailboat was larger than ours, yet she singlehandedly steered, navigated, and hauled up the sails. Over Christmas she visited her adult children in Chicago, always returning to her boat for the rest of the year, ready for the next Atlantic crossing. No seniors' retirement home for this lady.

Another woman I met lived with her teenaged son on a sailboat not far from our marina slip. No husband or male partner in sight. She made her living by donning diving gear and scrubbing the hulls of sailboats at the docks. How, I wanted to know, had fate brought her to this style of living? Did she enjoy her life? It was free but so physically demanding. Did she worry about the future? In this marina I learned how bravely people lived out their untypical lives. I realized how sheltered I had been from economic hardship and the prospect of a life lived separate from the mainstream of society. For some, such a solo, independent existence is a dream: the reality strikes me as a bit of a nightmare.

On New Year's Eve, Fraser and I sat in the cockpit of *Greensleeves* and watched fireworks explode over the night skyline of Miami. Shouts of jubilation could be heard from other boats along the dock welcoming in the new millennium. After Fraser went below to sleep, I lingered in the cockpit to take in the quiet end of a noisy evening. As the black water lapped against the hull, I poured myself a third glass of chilled Sancerre and settled into the cockpit cushions. I pondered on the changes in my life over the last four years: a move from Toronto, Canada's largest city, to a fishing village on the Aspotogan Peninsula. I had no idea of what lay ahead for me and Fraser in 2000.

The voyage on *Greensleeves* had been exhilarating, the opportunity of a lifetime. I had now lived the full geographic spectrum, from the complexity of a major city to the simplicity of a seaside village. Still, at my core I remained essentially unchanged, but perhaps stronger. On the other hand, the outer material world changed constantly. Yet all the change and moving about and the dramatic, tragic, and joyous happenings seemed to lead nowhere in particular. Was life a tale "told by an idiot, full of sound and fury, signifying nothing" as Shakespeare claimed? I wasn't yet ready to subscribe to the great man's dark view. I still hoped to find a Something-Other-Than that would prove to be changeless, totally consuming, and supportive. I needed to explore my inner life more fully to see what answers might lie within.

Fraser's dream of blue sailing the Atlantic came with a cost, as most dreams do. About to enter our sixth decade, we were temporarily homeless and unemployed, with little cash-on-hand, a situation not unlike the early days of our marriage—looking for a job and a place to call home. Simple needs, but sometimes difficult to achieve.

Sitting on *Greensleeves* while watching the Miami skyline, I brushed aside these practical concerns. It was time to take pleasure in what we had accomplished. We would figure out a way through the nitty gritty of survival. For now, I admired our daring feat of sailing down the Eastern Seaboard of North America. Hope and enthusiasm for the spiritual quest filled me once again. I was finally out of the doldrums, and I could feel the wind in my sails pulling me forward.

SIX:

THE WAY OF THE DREAM

SIX:

THE WAY OF THE DREAM

After our return to Toronto from Miami, I was ready to step over another threshold in my life's journey. At sixty, I had completed three of life's major tasks—the finding of a life partner, the bearing and raising of children, and the acquisition of the skills needed to earn a living. One task remained unfinished: coming to a perspective on the purpose of my existence and whether another level of being exists after death. After decades of looking, I had come to no firm conclusion. An unequivocal experience of the divine embedded in human existence still eluded me. I viewed that Something-Other-Than through a very dark glass.

Later, I found my mood reflected in the opening lines of the Italian poet Dante Alighieri's long narrative poem *The Divine Comedy*, which traces Dante's journey from darkness to the divine light:

> Midway along the journey of our life
>> I woke to find myself in a dark wood,
>> For I had wandered off from the straight path.
>
> How hard it is to tell what it was like,

This wood of wilderness, savage and stubborn
(The thought of it brings back all my
old fears),

A bitter place! Death could scarce be bitterer.
But if I would show the good that came of it
I must talk about things other than
the good.[31]

My mindset wasn't quite as dire as the one described by Dante. I wasn't so much bitter as disappointed in the discrepancy between what I had aspired to achieve in my spiritual quest and what I had accomplished. I had let financial considerations and a career push aside the disciplines required for yoga and poetry. At a physical survival level, these pressures were real, and attention needed to be paid. But perhaps not for such long stretches of time. I had wandered from my chosen spiritual path. Like Dante, my soul had become lost in the woods. Now it was time to look for another way through the wilderness.

I didn't have far to look for another spiritual path. During my time as a disciple of Yogi Desai, I had encountered the work of the Swiss psychologist Carl Gustav Jung, who would become my second spiritual guru. He came to have a profound effect on my subsequent thinking, so much so that I can remember the exact moment when I encountered his life in a bookstore located in Cranleigh, a village in Surrey, England, not far from our home village of Peaslake.

It was a spring afternoon in 1981. The daffodils in the village square were shimmering in the intensity of their yellowness. My errands completed, I decided to indulge myself with a browse through the village bookstore. After passing through the

---

31. Dante Alighieri, *The Divine Comedy* (New York: Penguin Books, 2013), 67.

fiction, cookery, and gardening sections, my eyes came to rest on a Penguin paperback in the biography section titled *Jung and the Story of Our Time*, written by Laurens van der Post, the South African author, explorer, and political advisor to British heads of state. I was familiar with van der Post's name, having seen him featured in a television documentary. But the man he was writing about—Carl Gustav Jung—was only a name to me. His life and work had not pierced my bubble of awareness.

I read the blurb on the back of van der Post's book and skimmed the first chapter. I was immediately hooked. Here was an account of a person who spoke of the things that intrigued me on my quest. I took the biography home to our cottage in the Surrey woods, where I devoured its contents and acquainted myself with the life and thought of C. G. Jung.

Jung's life story as told by Laurens van der Post revealed a man like no other. Initially, Jung was recognized in popular culture as a psychologist and psychiatrist, a healer of mental suffering. But van der Post showed how Jung's work extended well beyond that of a mental healer to embrace the development of the internal spiritual self. Jung held the view that all mental and emotional problems were, at their source, a question of regaining a religious attitude that had nothing to do with creeds or belonging to a church.

I found the best way to orient myself to Jung's work and character was to read his memoir, *Memories, Dreams, Reflections*.[32] Jung's interests were encyclopedic. Besides being a man of medical science, he didn't hesitate to venture into borderline areas like alchemy, astrology, dreams, the unconscious, and the soul. Taking on these esoteric subjects earned him intense criticism from his medical colleagues in the developing field of

---

32. C. G. Jung, *Memories, Dreams, Reflections* (New York: Random House, 1989).

psychology. Until I connected with Jung's work, I held a dim view of the field of psychology. At university I had enrolled in a course taught by a renowned psychologist of the time. I found the lectures boring beyond belief. They focused on how mice navigated mazes in a laboratory when an electric shock was applied to the poor rodents' backsides. The range of Jung's work opened my mind to a more exciting perspective on human psychology.

It's not possible to speak of a spiritual journey without referencing the concept of the soul, sometimes spoken of as the Self. I've already used the word several times without a rigorous definition, mainly because its meaning is ambiguous at best. In general, the fields of religion and philosophy consider the soul to be the immaterial aspect or essence of a human being, that which confers individuality and humanity on an individual. Soul is tied to life in all its particulars—good food, satisfying conversation, close friends, and experiences that remain in the memory and touch the heart. One scholar referred to the soul as the vital, mysterious, and wild core of our individual selves, much deeper than our personalities.

The soul can be defined from three points of view, that of theology, philosophy, and psychology, which tends to blur the definition even more. Despite the uncertainty surrounding the concept of soul, C. G. Jung did not shy away from its use in his writing and thinking. The concept of soul has a long historical pedigree, beginning with the ancient Egyptian notion of *ka* (breath) and the early Greek schools of philosophy, including the Epicureans, the Platonists, and even Aristotle. The Hindu and Islamic religions also include the soul as an aspect of their theology, although they call it by different names with slightly different attributes. In ancient times, the soul was thought to join the ranks of the venerated ancestors in the Underworld. It was at the point of visualizing such an Underworld that the longing for eternal salvation and the fear of eternal damnation consumed humanity, especially in the Christian tradition.

Does the soul have any materiality? Opinions vary. Some Greek philosophers considered the soul to be made up of atoms like the rest of the body, while other schools of thought concluded the soul was an immaterial and incorporeal substance, akin to the gods yet part of the world of change and becoming. Modern philosophy doesn't envisage soul as a substance but as a subjectivity, intuition, a feeling, or taste for the infinite.

In Christian theology, the soul refers to the divine essence of an individual that survives the death of the body to join in an afterlife of heaven or hell. This belief can't be proved by anyone, as those who die do not come back to tell us the truth of the matter. Still, I prefer to entertain the possibility of an afterlife. It soothes my fears of complete extinction at death of all that I consider myself to be. Ironically, in recent times a belief in an afterlife has lost its credibility, resulting in what religious commentators and some creative writers have called a loss of the soul, the chronic ailment of contemporary culture. Today, philosophers and psychologists avoid the concept of soul, preferring more scientific-sounding terms like "the subjective aspect of human life," "thinking matter," and "psyche." They leave the use of the word *soul* to poets, musicians, painters, sculptors, and other artists.

After "meeting" Jung in the Surrey bookstore, I spent the next fifteen years intermittently reading his works and commentaries by psychoanalysts who applied his concepts in their practice. Jung's writings are complex, and I confess to having understood only about 60 per cent of what I read. Nevertheless, I stuck with him because I sensed there was something worth knowing here. Usually when I enter a terrain of knowledge about which

I know nothing, I find repeated readings gradually build my understanding, until one day the light switch turns on and my comprehension soars.

Jung's colleagues are exceptional in their ability to explain to the layman the complexities of his theories and terminology. One of the best is June Singer, who wrote *Boundaries of the Soul: The Practice of Jung's Psychology*. She clarified the dizzying array of Jungian concepts, including the unconscious, introversion/extroversion, archetypes, the psyche, individuation, persona, shadow, anima, animus, the Self, and active imagination. I wouldn't presume to explain these concepts here in the detail and with the sophistication they deserve. Instead, I will limit myself to three terms relevant to my story.

Psyche is an essential term when dealing with Jung's ideas; it refers to the entire mental apparatus of the human mind, including the conscious and the unconscious. In common parlance, the term *mind* designates only the conscious aspect of mental functioning. Conceived as the tip of the psychic iceberg, consciousness refers to human behaviour, which is motivated and largely determined by a person's conscious personality. In other words, we are conscious of what we are doing and why. The *ego* is the focal point of consciousness and bears our continuing sense of personal identity. The *Self*, as employed by Jung, refers to a state or force much greater than the ego. Jung viewed the ego as orbiting the Self like the Earth orbits the sun. On the other hand, portions of the psyche are not directly accessible to consciousness and so are referred to as the unconscious. The existence of such a mind aspect cannot be decisively proven but only inferred from its manifestation in symbols, symptoms, and actions. Still, it remains a useful hypothesis in the hands of a skilled analyst. Although unrealized to most people, these unconscious energies produce a deep effect on our conscious thoughts and actions. For the psychologist and psychiatrist, their importance in understanding a patient cannot be overstated.

According to Jung, the mental health (or illness) of a person depends on achieving a functional relationship between the unconscious and conscious factions of the mind. The task of the analyst is to work with the client to readjust this relationship when it malfunctions. So far, the hypothesis of the existence of an unconscious has served psychology well as a cultural shorthand to speak of complicated mental states.

Given the crucial importance of the unconscious, Jung committed himself religiously to the recording and comprehension of images and symbols arising from the unconscious inner life of the individual. In the opening paragraph of his memoir, Jung makes this statement of his life's meaning: "My life is a story of the self-realization of the unconscious."[33] His goal was to seek the divine through illuminating the inaccessible activities and processes of the unconscious where, in his view, all meaning originated.

Jung turned to dreams as the most crucial avenue to an understanding of the forces and energies at work in his unconscious. By looking at his dreams carefully, reflecting on them, and plumbing their images for meaning, he felt he could come to know the contents of his unconscious. He rejected other techniques such as hypnosis, free association, automatic writing, and past lives to focus on his dreams. He wrote about his confrontation with his unconscious in *The Red Book*, published after his death. He considered the results the primary resource for deriving his theories. He advised his clients to create their own version of *The Red Book*, which would become a personal bible to guide them in the way of their own souls.

---

33. C. G. Jung, *Memories, Dreams, Reflections*, 3.

I was enthusiastic about Jung's idea of using dreams to understand one's unconscious. Whatever I discovered through my dreams would reflect *my* dreams and *my* psyche, not an extension of someone else's thoughts and beliefs. In this manner, I could stay close to my true nature and not be dragged off into religious dogma or esoteric spiritual schemes.

My switch from the guidance of an Eastern guru to the interpretations of a Western psychoanalyst was not a trivial matter. Jung wrote an entire book about the effects on the Western psyche of practising Eastern spiritual traditions titled *Psychology and the East*. He claimed the Indian mentality forged over four thousand uninterrupted years of yoga precepts and disciplines evolved along entirely different lines from the Christian and Judaic theologies. In his view, the psychic makeup of the Westerner and the Easterner was so different as to render the practice of yoga incompatible with the Western psyche. Jung didn't criticize yoga per se but rather directed his criticism against the application of yoga to peoples of the West.

I'm sure Jung's view of the differences between the psyche of the Easterner and the Westerner is controversial, but I find his view provides a possible explanation of why I had such difficulty quieting my mind in meditation. I often felt I didn't want my mind to be quiet. In most instances, I enjoyed the variability of my thoughts, which flitted through my mind like brilliant tropical birds in a forest. In contrast, yogic texts refer to the mind as a mischievous monkey that needs to be disciplined. *Monkey mind*, yoga practitioners will say, is the greatest challenge to spiritual progress. I'm not sure I agree.

The Eastern mind is comfortable with the fusing together of mind and body resulting in a wholeness of body and spirit. These traditions seek to calm the mind, to remove the vestiges of the contents in the unconscious through meditation, whereas Western tradition values the contents of the unconscious. For this reason, psychologists consider dreams an important part of understanding the mind. Not so the Easterner. I recall hearing Yogi Desai disparage dreams, insisting they signified nothing. Here is Jung's view of the effect of yoga on the European mind:

> [Western man's psychic disposition] is quite different from that of the Oriental. I say to whomever I can: Study yoga—you will learn an infinite amount from it—but do not try to apply it, for we Europeans are not so constituted that we apply these methods correctly, just like that. An Indian guru can explain everything and you can imitate everything. But do you know *who* is applying the yoga? In other words, do you know who you are and how you are constituted?[34]

Until I reached my thirties, I hadn't taken my dreams very seriously. Every so often, a particularly forceful dream would pique my interest and I'd discuss it with a friend. But the discussion was always light-hearted and of the cocktail-party variety. They came, created a bit of a mental fuss, then most often disappeared from memory. Conventional attitudes viewed dreams as mental mumbo-jumbo spewed out by a tired brain at the end of a day. Not so for Jung and his colleague Sigmund Freud, who famously said that dreams were the "royal road to the unconscious." Jung considered dreams to be "documents of the soul" written in the "language of the soul."

At this point, I began to keep a log of my dreams as a complement to the spiritual disciplines I'd learned through yoga. While I found it intriguing to read them over and speculate on

---

34. C. G. Jung, *Psychology and the East* (Princeton: Princeton University Press, 1978), 82.

what they meant, I needed help to decipher their significance. Each dream seemed disconnected from the others. I was floundering in images and strange dramatic plots that my logical mind couldn't absorb. Perhaps a Jungian analyst could help.

Undertaking dreamwork with a Jungian analyst seemed an appropriate transition to the next step in my spiritual quest. In my reading I found multiple warnings about the power of the unconscious to disrupt one's normal mental functions. It was always recommended to find someone skilled in dreamwork as a guide through the rough episodes. Jung had struggled to confront his unconscious through his dreams. While he met with considerable success, it took many years of intense study, and he suffered a mental crisis in the process. I preferred to avoid such an eventuality if possible.

How does one go about locating an analyst, a stranger who will be privy to your innermost secrets, who might hold the key to opening your soul to infinite possibilities of spirit? No one in my circle of friends and acquaintances had ever admitted to using the services of an analyst, let alone a Jungian analyst. I don't think many even considered the possibility.

I began my search on the website of the C. G. Jung Foundation of Ontario, the organization charged with promoting the study of Jung's work and the training of Jungian analysts. From a lineup of headshots on the foundation's website, I selected at random a man in his early forties who had studied at the C. G. Jung Institute in Zurich, Switzerland, and held a master's in social work from the University of Toronto. For this memoir I've given him the name Ron.

In the early evening of December 6, 2000, I nervously pressed the buzzer in the lobby of a three-storey apartment building downtown, which had been converted into office units. I announced myself and was buzzed through the foyer door. I walked down a dim, carpeted corridor to a door where the number "213" appeared in raised brass.

Ron stood up as I entered, shook my hand, and we exchanged introductions. He gestured for me to sit in an armchair while he sat in a black leather chair facing mine. He waited in silence while I arranged my purse and tote bag at my feet.

Once settled, I glanced around the room. The distance between Ron's chair and mine was too far for an intimate conversation, but I instinctively knew it was calculated to create a psychic space that was friendly but not invasive of one's personal space. At least I was spared the Freudian cliché of lying on a couch with Ron sitting out of sight behind me.

I was vaguely aware of a colourful abstract painting on the wall and a weeping fig tree to the right of Ron's chair. The lower leaves looked limp and ready to drop, perhaps overwhelmed by what the tree heard in the room every day. The coffee table between us held a squat yellow candle, a box of tissues, and a small clock with its face turned away from me. Ah yes, the clock was ticking. The session would only last one hour.

Finally, I focused my attention on Ron. In my reading of Jung's work, the relationship between analyst and analysand was deemed critical to the success of the analysis. This initial meeting would set the tone for subsequent sessions. Ron was of medium height, probably in his early forties, with an athletic build and brown hair in a partial buzz cut. He sported the recently fashionable unshaven look, which in my younger years had signified an unemployed man down on his luck and too fond of alcoholic spirits. He was dressed informally in jeans and carried a backpack, which lay at his feet. He smiled rather awkwardly. Ron was not what I expected an analyst to look like. I was unduly influenced by photographs I'd seen of an older Jung, which showed a relaxed, grandfatherly figure with snow white hair, immaculately dressed, and radiating the demeanour and confidence of a wise man. In contrast, Ron presented as a tense youngish man with dark hair and a brooding sense of social unease about him.

In our first session we talked about why I was there. What issue had brought me into analysis, who were the major players in my daily life, and what role he could play in helping me. I told him about my husband and two sons and my widowed mother. "But I'm *not* looking for a cure for a neurosis or advice on a malfunctioning relationship," I said. "I'm a spiritual seeker." I wanted to discover for myself, I continued, if the unconscious was a manifestation of the God within and if my dreams were the way to make contact. I wanted to connect with that invisible unconscious force called the Godhead. It would be a bonus, but not essential, if he were also able to shed light on the difficulties of my relationship with my mother.

Ron agreed we would have a dialogue with my unconscious through the dreams I'd bring each session. By the end of the analysis, I could expect to feel more balanced within myself, less introverted, and more open to emotional connection. As to how long the process would take, it was impossible to say. The sessions would take place once a week with a few breaks over the summer and at Christmas.

I didn't say anything to Ron at the time, but I was hoping for much more from dream analysis than feeling emotionally balanced. In metaphorical terms, I wanted to see the biblical burning bush, to have an insight into the universe, to encounter the Great One who runs this cosmic circus of infinite mystery. My ultimate expectations were absurdly high, but I would see how far Ron and Jungian dream analysis could take me. I was willing to pay the price in time as well as dollars if I could sleep better and rid myself of the free-floating anxiety that made a good night's sleep a challenge.

In Jungian analysis, the first dreams brought to the analyst are given particular attention. The theory is that they encapsulate the underlying problem and predict the direction the analysis is likely to take. These are the first two dreams I brought to my analysis with Ron. The dreams occurred on the same night.

Dream #1: Airplane Crash

My husband and I are in a marketplace in North Africa. We board an airplane, but the engine gives trouble. In spite of technical difficulties, we land safely and board a second airplane, which also gets into mechanical trouble. A voice over the intercom says we are going to die. I accept this verdict.

The plane hits the ground and spins out of control, going in circles and crashing into other planes on the runway. Pieces of debris streak past the window. I think, *This is what it's like to die.* Suddenly, it's quiet and the airplane stops moving. A voice says we are still alive.

My husband and I get out of the airplane through a large gaping hole in its side. We meet friends at the airport, which is still in Africa. I'm eager to tell our friends about our close call, but the airport is so crowded I can only shout, "We had a close call," without going into details.

We move through the airport. At one point I see racks full of videos for rent. I marvel at their appearance in this foreign airport and think how parents could use the videos to amuse their children in a hotel room.

Dream #2: Silver Fish

I'm standing on a dock where children, mostly boys, are having fun jumping into the water. A young man gently asks them not to run on the dock.

From the edge of the dock, I look down into the water, which is part of a river. The water is murky and filled with small fish with silver scales and circular bodies. I consider jumping into the water with the fish, but I'm afraid. I ask the young man in a joking fashion if adults can jump into the water. He laughs and says, "Of course."

Ron took the lead in analyzing these two dreams, as I was at a loss as to how to extract any meaning out of this "imaginary" set of events. I was surprised to see my husband taking on such a major role in this dream drama. Ron quickly viewed the airplane as an enclosed container representative of our marriage relationship. The crash indicated the status quo in our marriage could not survive; it had lost altitude and could no longer take us where we want to go. And yet we survive the crash and escape the confines of the airplane (our marriage). When we exit the airplane, we find ourselves still in Africa. Despite the barren surroundings, the country is a nourishing, friendly place, a good place to be. The mention of children at the end of the dream signifies the presence of new life. Something is waiting to be reborn. The unconscious is conveying through the dream that our marriage will survive this crisis.

This example clearly illustrates the subjective nature of ascribing a dream image to stand in for something utterly different in real life. While Ron chose to equate the airplanes with my marriage, I didn't read the dream that way at all. For me the airplanes represented spiritual conveyances for descending from the Upper world to the Underworld. This conflict in interpretating a dream happened several times during our analytical sessions. In this instance, Ron conceded the crashing airplanes could signify a descent to the Underworld rather than a troubled marriage. But he didn't entirely let go of his initial interpretation, as would become obvious in future sessions.

The second dream continues the motif of children that appears at the end of the first dream. According to Ron, the water beneath the dock represents the river of life, the unconscious, where the children are at play and eager to jump in. This image signifies my desire to enter analysis while reflecting a hesitancy to take the plunge. The water in the dream is murky, like the unconscious, but bright, circular fish are swimming in the water, their natural environment. The images of these silver, incandescent fish evoked in me a sense of beauty, mystery, and vitality. Fish have long stood as a powerful mythological symbol with connections to astrology, the unconscious, and to Christianity. For instance, Christians portrayed converts awaiting baptism as fish swimming around the ankles of Christ, Christ called his disciples "fishers of men," and he fed 5,000 followers with two fishes and five loaves of bread. Before the Christian age, the Greeks, Romans, and pagans considered the fish to be a symbol of fertility.

Ron said these two dreams were connected and quite reassuring. From the perspective of mythology, he conceded the descent of the airplanes from the sky in the first dream might represent the descent into the Underworld of my unconscious. The follow-up dream ends with me standing on a dock and peering into the surface of the water, a common image for the unconscious. The multitude of fishes swimming about are reflective of spiritual matters. According to Ron, the overall direction of this second dream is to encourage me to overcome my fears and dive into my unconscious. My ego is ready yet cautious about engaging in a direct conversation with such a powerful and mysterious entity.

After the session I left Ron's office deep in thought about our dialogue, especially the luminescent silver fish in my dream. As I walked toward the subway station, a white panel truck turned onto the street from a side road and drove past. The words "CITY FISH" in bold black letters on the side of the truck caught my attention immediately. Seeing the word "FISH" so soon after analyzing my dream about fish seemed like a sign of sorts. I associated the other word, "CITY," as designating that the fish were marooned in the dry materialism of city life. An inner certitude told me the timing of these two separate events was more than just a coincidence. Jung named this sort of occurrence *synchronicity*, where two or more random events happen in a way suggesting something other than chance is involved. As an example, one night Jung dreamt of a kingfisher bird with its iridescent turquoise blue and orange plumage. The next morning, he found a kingfisher dead in his garden, an extremely rare species of bird never seen before or since in that region of Switzerland.

As I continued walking toward the subway, which now seemed to be a symbolic Underworld, I realized my dream analysis was taking place not far from the house where I had lived as an eight-year-old child. As well, a half-block from Ron's office I passed the church where I had attended Brownies at the age of ten. It was here I made my first stand for independence by not waiting for my mother to walk me home. When my mother arrived at the church and I wasn't there, she was understandably frightened. I walked home alone, proud of my new-found independence. When she arrived home to find me safe and happy, her mixture of anger and relief caused her to tell me how I had missed out on the ice cream treat she planned to buy me on the way home. Independence, I learned, had its price.

On my way home to the suburbs after my first session of dreamwork, I sat in the subway car and pondered the possibility that my dream life and my waking life were about to coalesce into a constellation of dream and reality.

———————

Analyzing dreams is an intuitive and instinctual calling, more an art than a science. Unlike other scientists, psychoanalysts are obliged to use the same tool (the psyche) to study the object being studied (also the psyche). In the words of one Jungian analyst, "We are ourselves the mystery which we are seeking to unravel." This difficulty requires deploying methods used more in poetry, storytelling, magic, and rituals than in scientific matters.

During the four years I spent doing dreamwork with Ron, I logged three hundred dreams. Some weeks I had no new dreams to discuss, and some weeks there would be too many to cover in our hourly session. When I started out, I knew nothing of dream interpretation. The literature was overwhelming. Eventually, I winnowed the titles down to three, all written by well-known Jungian analysts: Robert Johnson's *Inner Work: Using Dreams & Active Imagination for Personal Growth*, Anthony Stevens's *Private Myths: Dreams and Dreaming*, and James Hillman's *The Dream and the Underworld*. From these sources I was able to orient myself to the process of dream analysis as applied by Jungian analysts.

The first step is to write down the details of the dreams and list their images and symbols to find out what personal and cultural associations they have for the dreamer. Selecting these associations is the most tricky and subjective stage of the process. It provides the foundation for the final stage where the dream, now amplified by personal and mythological associations, is placed within the context of the dreamer's life situation and psychological state. There is some dispute about this stage of dream interpretation. Not all Jungian analysts consider dreams to be solely related to the dreamer's personal life. The unconscious may generate images from the invisible inner world of the mind and the imagination, which are not necessarily connected to a person's daily life.

Dreaming can't be boiled down into a cut-and-dried information-processing activity. Jung referred to dreams as inspirations. He and other analysts considered dreams to be highly creative products of the imagination, where the dream digests bits and pieces from the day and converts them into images. Jung felt there was a strong connection between dreams and poetry in their similar emphasis on images and the metaphoric language employed. He often used to quote three lines from the W. H. Auden poem "In Memory of Ernst Toller" where he illustrated the power of this inner genius within our psyches:

> We are lived by powers we pretend to understand:
> They arrange our loves; it is they who direct at the end
> The enemy bullet, the sickness, or even our hand.[35]

Every morning throughout my dream analysis I wrote down the images and dramatic actions in my dreams before the details faded away. Dreams can vanish from memory within minutes of awakening. Besides noting the content of the dream, I briefly wrote down the highlights of the previous day and the tenor of my feelings. This served as an aid in linking the nighttime dream to my daytime reality.

Ron and I would review the images in each dream and try to see what associations they triggered in me. Each dream turned

---

35. W. H. Auden, *The Complete Works of W. H. Auden: Poems, vol. II 1940–1974.* (Princeton, New Jersey: Princeton University Press, 2022.)

into a puzzle, a mystery to be solved. The process of analyzing the dream ignited an exciting urge to find the solution. Whatever one thinks of the ultimate value of dreams, it's remarkable how the unconscious creates such a wide range of startling images and situations. Yes, dreams can be nonsensical and frustratingly disjointed and defy every physical law of daytime reality. But at the same time, they demonstrate a unique genius beyond what's apparent in our daytime life.

The literature on dream analysis is vast and holds much complexity and seeming contradictions. Even after reading widely and having gone through dream analysis with an analyst, I don't consider myself a skilled interpreter of dreams. That level of accomplishment would take years of academic study. For this memoir, I'm only able to pass on the process of dream analysis as I experienced it.

In the second month of our collaboration, we worked on a dream I labelled "Dark Skies."

Dark Skies

The sky is dark with a rainstorm threatening. I run toward the storm, holding a piece of paper in my hand while looking for a wastepaper basket. A voice says, "Here it comes." The sky grows even darker.

I turn and run from the storm. I look over my shoulder and see sheets of water rolling off the roof of a Tudor-style house and streaming down the front windows. I rush away to find shelter before the storm catches up with me. (*January 17, 2001*)

Six images dominate this dream—a dark sky, a storm, a Tudor house, sheets of water, a piece of paper, and the spoken words "here it comes." Each image offers a portal to explore the dream's meaning. Given the limitation of our one-hour session, Ron and I focused on four of the most significant—a dark sky, a storm, a Tudor house, and the sheet of water.

Ron asked me what personal associations each image activated in my mind. An association could be a word, an idea, a feeling, or a memory—whatever came spontaneously to mind, no matter how illogical or bizarre. Predictably, I associated a *dark sky* and a *storm* with chaos and imminent danger based on a childhood memory of a summer storm that caused the roof of our cottage to leak, making me fear for my life. The *Tudor house* was associated with happy memories of family life lived in two houses with Tudor facades.

Sheets of water did not immediately elicit an association, due to the ubiquity of water images in many dreams. In a dream the image of water can suggest the presence of both the unconscious and death. High waves of water can indicate an overwhelming, threatening emotion. In everyday life, *water* can be a giver of life as well as a bringer of death. Pour water on a plant shrivelled and dehydrated by lack of water and within hours its leaves and blooms will swell with life. Alternatively, if you place people in the path of a raging river overflowing its banks, these people may drown. Ten days without water of any kind and humans can die of dehydration.

Given the many ways to interpret *sheets of water* in this dream sequence, how does a dreamer know which association is the right one? The atmosphere and the context of the dream certainly influence the choice, but in many cases an emotional reaction to an association, such as a mental click or a shiver down the spine, signifying an "Aha" moment, may point in the right direction. The subjective nature of associations requires the analyst and the dreamer to embrace a degree of uncertainty and mystery for what lies at the core of the human psyche. Some analysts have said that if you arrive at an interpretation of a dream too quickly, you've probably missed the meaning. Some meanings do not solidify for months or even years, which is why analysts discourage the over-reliance on books of standardized interpretations of dream images.

After much discussion, I came to associate the *sheet of water* in my dream with a threat to my family life, as represented by the Tudor house about to be swept away by the water. At the time of this dream, my two adult sons had recently left home to start their own lives, and I was in the throes of suffering from empty nest syndrome. I experienced this leave-taking as a death of sorts, for I dearly loved my family life.

Having determined my associations with the images in "Dark Skies," we entered the third and final stage of analyzing the dream by considering how these images and their associations lined up with my current life. After some reflection, Ron and I concluded that the dream represented my emotional reaction to starting analysis. The dream was warning me that going into analysis presented a potential threat to my family life. The approaching storm indicated the emotional turmoil that analysis would likely trigger. Despite my professed eagerness to proceed with dream analysis, Ron suggested my turning and running from the storm reflected my fear of the process and an unconscious holding back from proceeding. I went along with his interpretation, not because I was sure it was the right one, but because I couldn't think of another explanation that fit better.

At home I would make notes on what had transpired during our session. I considered each session to be a conversation or dialogue, not a forum for Ron's opinions. I was not averse to offering up another interpretation if the one he put forward didn't feel right. In the beginning of our time together, I was more open to his interpretations, as this dream analysis activity was new to me. But in time, I looked on each session as a mutual exchange of views, allowing that Ron might have better insight for being outside my situation and trained in the significance of dream images.

The dreams that most caught my attention were those that repeated the same imagery over a long period of time. A common motif in my dreams is being chased by malevolent beings, either animal or human, who snap and snarl at my heels. In several dreams I answer a knock at my door to find several men dressed in black ready to abduct me. "Grab her," they say in ominous tones. I slam the door shut and retreat into the house.

The most repetitive and terrifying of my dreams concerns the theme of going blind. I am alone in a car and driving at night on a country road when suddenly I go blind and can't stop the car. The car continues at high speed throughout the night. I cannot see the road. Frequently, a sense of terror ejects me from my sleeping state into being wide awake. In another dream I am a young child who swallows a razor blade. I peer at myself in a mirror but do nothing to take the razor blade out of my mouth. The dream doesn't present a reason for such a bizarre action. The sensation of choking on a razor blade stays in my memory to this day.

Many of my dreams circled around the theme of losing my purse. For women, a purse holds intimate objects related to her identity (wallet, driver's licence, money, lipstick, rouge, comb). These dream scenes always take place in wide-open public spaces where I'm trying to get somewhere and several obstacles prevent me from forging ahead, one of which is the loss of my purse. In metaphorical terms, this repetitive dream would show me as always seeking something and failing due to a loss of my inner identity, maybe my soul—the ultimate source of my identity.

It's been widely observed that dreams are preponderantly unpleasant, encouraging a view of them as by-products of an underworld of darkness, ghosts, and death. Some Jungian analysts have gone so far as to claim the goal of dreams is to prepare the dreamer for death. I can't say if this is so, except to remark that very few of my dreams are explicitly happy. In one of my maybe eight happy dreams, I'm standing on a hilltop, gazing in wonder at a shimmering tree covered with white flowers. The tree radiates pure love. The reassuring sense of being surrounded by love was still with me when I awoke, and it lingered for weeks.

———————

Jung developed a technique to supplement dreams and plunge deeper into the unconscious. He called it *active imagination (AI)*, a conscious form of interaction with the figures, plots, and moods of a dream. As he describes it in his memoir, the process begins by taking slow, meditative breaths as you imagine a steep descent, all the while focusing on an image or person from a recent dream; alternatively, you simply observe what images arise spontaneously from the unconscious. These images represent deep interior parts of yourselves. You engage in a dialogue and interact with these aspects of yourself using the faculty of your imagination. Surprisingly, in this dreamlike state the figures and images, when questioned, will answer back. Often they'll express radically different viewpoints from those of the conscious mind. You record this fantasy dialogue with pen, paper, or Dictaphone.

Jung considered active imagination to be an even more effective path to the unconscious than dreams. He called the results of this activity *conscious fantasies* or just *fantasies*. He was adamant the technique was not a passive acceptance of what the unconscious puts forth but a critical cross-examination of what the actors in the dream insist on as evidence of their point of view. He would talk back to his fantasies.

I was immediately drawn to active imagination as a technique because Jung placed such a high value on its ability to access the contents of the unconscious. He used active imagination to confront his own unconscious, writing down and profusely illustrating the fantasies arising from this confrontation. These revealing fantasies were published after his death in *The Red Book*, which he referred to as "the bible of my soul."

Facing his unconscious in this manner carried a risk. There was a chance the resulting fantasies could have taken over Jung's conscious mind and pushed him toward madness, which he claimed had happened to a few other philosophers and thinkers. I had no fears there, as I was in analysis with a professional Jungian who could spot any problems with my ability to cope with reality. I was disappointed when Ron said he couldn't advise me on active imagination. He didn't understand the technique and couldn't make it work for him. He agreed to listen to the fantasies that occurred during my AI sessions and be alert to any dramatic shift in my thought processes, but he couldn't actively advise on the process. I was on my own.

I turned to Robert Johnson's book *Inner Work* to guide me through the process of active imagination. He clearly lays out the steps of active imagination in non-threatening terms. In the second year of my analysis, I experienced an AI dialogue that triggered an intense tingling in the middle of my forehead, considered by yogis to be the third eye, the gateway to the inner realms of higher consciousness. Not all my AI sessions produced this physical symptom, but its frequent occurrence led me to take active imagination seriously as a way into the unconscious.

In one AI session, after settling into a meditative state of mind, I watched the following scenario play out in my mind, as if on a stage:

> I am in a grand ballroom in a European castle with high ceilings covered with gold gilt. A magnificent marble staircase descends into the ballroom. I walk down the staircase dressed in a white and gold flowing gown. I wear a diamond tiara on my head.
>
> At the bottom of the staircase stands a group of monks. A monk in the front row steps forward, smiles, and bows to me. I engage in a dialogue with him in the character of a part of myself I label the Queen. The monk opens the dialogue:
>
> **The Monk**: *When you are away, Queen, life loses much of its sparkle and zest. The people go about their daily tasks, but at heart they feel something vital is missing in their lives. That something special is what you bring to the kingdom.*
>
> The Queen looks pleasantly surprised by what the monk says. Lately, she has been unsure of her status as queen and seeks assurance of her usefulness to her kingdom.
>
> **The Monk**: *True royalty never dies,* continues the Monk. *The divinity in all of us finds expression in your personage. The people love that. They recognize the divinity in you. They need it in their lives; they want it. Speak with your people and tell them how much you love them.*

The Queen apologizes to her people for having neglected them for so long. While she may wear fancy jewelled shoes and long, flowing gowns, she feels the simple brown cloaks worn by her people remind her of the earth, the source that converts the seed of life into life-giving products such as fruit, vegetables, and animals.

The Queen: I feed off the fruits of your labour. I need to realize that more every day. Without you I cannot live a day.

Her people reassure her that they work so hard from sunup to sundown, sometimes getting sick and many of them dying, but it's done for the royal vision, the divine vision that makes it all worthwhile. The only thing they ask of her is not to hide in her castle but to be with them and talk to them of the possibilities in life.

The Queen: I take your point. We will start today. I will instruct my staff to prepare a wonderful feast this evening on the back lawn of the estate beside the lake. You are all invited. You will see a great fountain there with two galloping horses in the middle. It will make a marvellous backdrop to the feast.

This session of active imagination put me in touch with a part of myself that I hadn't consciously realized. The queenly part of me doesn't indicate an ambitious desire to rule a kingdom and have people defer to me because of my social status. On the contrary, being of royal lineage represents the realization of beauty of purpose and strength of character, which may eventually become worthy of an inner veneration and love of self. I see the queen in this dialogue as trying to connect with the divine, to be worthy of the people in her kingdom, who in return want and need her to pass on to them this divine essence. The monk represents my spiritual counsellor, who is keeping me grounded in the humble, and joyful things of life here and now. I must not forget that the everyday is a part of the divine. I must stay connected with the humbler, less evolved aspects of myself. I admire how the dialogue reveals the uncertainty that lurks beath the surface of my "queenly" aspects.

For six months I used active imagination in concert with dream analysis. Ron was impressed with the outcomes of my conscious participation with an imaginative experience. I was pleased as well. The dialogues surprised me. I wasn't consciously making them up; they just appeared full blown. After the six months, I stopped active imagination, mostly for lack of time.

Jung considered psychotherapy and analysis to be as varied as the human individuals involved. There was no one-method-fits-all approach that would guarantee a solution to the analysand's problem. The analysis was a frank conversation between one human being and another, where the psyche of the analyst was every bit as critical for success as the analysand's. The analysis required a level of trust and psychic intimacy between the parties. At the same time, the sessions must remain as emotionally objective as possible, without unconscious emotional baggage from either partner sabotaging the analytic process.

As part of their professional training, Jungian analysts undergo analysis themselves to become aware of their emotional blind spots and avoid the twin pitfalls of transference from the analysand and countertransference in the case of the analyst. On these occasions, each party projects unconscious processes from their psyches onto each other. For example, a female analysand growing up under the strong influence of a critical, fault-finding father might transfer her fear of criticism to the analyst and reject his constructive suggestions or, on the other hand, fall into a state of romantic infatuation because the analyst is kind to her. At the same time, the male analyst may be subject to a past unconscious pattern where his mother or sister held undue influence over him, creating a tendency to be hostile to feminine power of any sort. According to Jung, the success or failure of an analysis is bound up with the nature of the transference and countertransference, another way of saying the success of the analysis depends on the character of those participating in the dialogue.

I would characterize my feelings about Ron as ambivalent. He possessed an unusual mix of traits. An aura of darkness and anger seemed to cling to his person, stemming perhaps from a childhood trauma. His career as a social worker required him to daily undertake many acts of kindness and empathy to those who had little in life. He told me about going to help a patient paint his apartment, as he was mentally unable to undertake the task. I came to think of Ron as a rebel with heart. One day he commented on a portrait of the pianist Glenn Gould, showing empathy and affection for the famous musician, not so much for his music but for his awkward character traits similar to his own.

Ron wasn't as overtly knowledgeable about mythology and Jungian thought as I had anticipated. I came into analysis expecting my analyst to be a sort of prototypical wise man, an intellectual like C. G. Jung, slightly stooped, with rimless glasses and a corona of white hair, whereas Ron was more of a sensation type and not comfortable with intellectual analysis. On one occasion, he told me I was the smartest person who had ever entered his consulting room. I was truly shocked by this statement, as I considered myself to be of a mediocre intelligence. We rarely, if ever, discussed Jung's theories in depth, although early on he lent me a book, the first in a series of bestselling books written by the Peruvian anthropologist Carlos Castaneda featuring a blend of shamanism, psychedelic drugs, and alternate realities encountered during his apprenticeship to an Indian sorcerer named Don Juan Matus. Ron was very moved by Castaneda's books. I suspect Don Juan's teachings were more in line with his psyche than were Jung's views.

My emotional reaction to Ron fluctuated between annoyance and physical attraction. He annoyed me with his persistence around interpreting my dreams in the context of my relationship to my husband. I had entered dreamwork for spiritual insights, not to have marriage counselling. My husband and I had a few rough spots in our relationship, mostly around communicating our needs clearly to one another. But in the grand scheme of things, the points of conflict were minor in degree—like flies at a picnic—momentary distractions that didn't spoil the meal. Ron referenced his ex-wife several times during our sessions. Perhaps this personal wound spurred the focus on my relationship with my husband.

And then midway through the analysis came the unexpected bouts of being physically attracted to Ron. I had read this attraction was not uncommon; it was part of the transference and countertransference between analyst and analysand. Even the great master Jung had given into this urge and slept with his analysands. I never let my attraction for Ron show, nor did he respond in any way that could be interpreted as flirting. Right from the beginning he told me he was always careful not to transgress this line of intimacy with an analysand. After several months, my attraction to him faded, and I was embarrassed that such craziness had possessed me.

To this day I question why I stayed in dreamwork analysis for such a long time. Four calendar years seems interminable, although four years in psychological time can seem like a moment. I think principally it was compelling to have someone to talk to who didn't have skin in the game, who wouldn't be too eager to stop my tears rather than get to the truth of the matter. A strong bond can form between two people when one is being listened to fully without a hidden agenda. Most people are bored by other people's dreams and will kindly, but quickly, turn the conversation to other topics. In the space created by the analytic process, my dreams were the reason for being together in that small room, and I was the centre of attention. Even though I had to pay for this privilege, it felt comforting and confidence-building.

The most compelling reason, however, for staying in analysis so long was the excitement and mystery of searching through my dreams for revelations or "messages" from my unconscious. I couldn't bear the idea of walking away from the sessions before the Big Reveal happened. During the period of working with Ron, my dream count increased greatly. I had never dreamed so much before. Something was happening. Each day I would enter his office feeling the thrill of anticipation. *Today will be the day*, I'd say to myself. *Today is the day when the mystery of that Something-Other-Than will be revealed.*

One day I arrived early for our appointment and spotted Ron loping toward his office building, coming from the other end of the street. He wore a red ski jacket with his backpack slung over one shoulder. As usual, he was dressed in jeans. He looked so young and so ordinary without a medical white coat to signify his expertise. *And this is the person*, I thought, *to whom I am confiding my soul's secrets. Does he have the wisdom and gravitas to carry this thing off?* I recalled watching the Canadian novelist and poet Margaret Atwood in a television interview expressing an interesting take on revealing secrets about oneself: "Telling all your personal secrets to someone is giving away all your beans." Was I weakening my inner strength by giving away my secrets to Ron, even if done in a professional capacity?

I pushed away my doubts, focusing instead on the fact that Ron had been analyzed by one of the most reputable analysts in the Toronto community of Jungian analysts. His credentials were sound. I decided to take the risk and keep on with my dreamwork. I had run out of alternatives. Finding my Something-Other-Than was proving more difficult than I had imagined. I stayed with the process lured on by the hope that enlightenment lay around the corner.

During my last session with Ron, we had a very spirited and authentic dialogue. I realized he knew more about me and what made me tick than any other person in the world. So, it seemed strange to just end these weekly dialogues, walk away, no looking back, no prospect of renewal in the future. But I knew it was the right time to part.

At the end of our last session, we shook hands as usual, and he wished me well on my solo journey. I felt moved to kiss him on the cheek but knowing how strongly he felt about keeping proper boundaries between analyst and analysand, I simply blew him a kiss. He smiled shyly and diverted his glance toward the floor. During the last fifteen years I've occasionally thought about him and our work together, but I never felt the need for refresher sessions.

Five years after I finished working with Ron, I decided to give dream analysis one more try, only this time with a woman. I had read that a female analyst might draw out different aspects of my psyche. I attended several sessions over a six-month period. The switch to a woman analyst was not a success. I found her manner officious and lacking in empathy. She had the annoying habit of reminding me how lucky I was to have her for an analyst. "I don't take just anyone," she would say, "but I think there is something I can do to help you." She frequently bungled the handling of invoices for her service, leaving me doubting her business ability.

Despite this lack of psychic connection between us, I continued to dream. Surprisingly, the themes in the dreams were often the same as with Ron. I still dreamed of losing my wallet and going blind while driving a car. Apparently, my psyche was still circling around the same issues without enlightening me as to their meaning. I could come up with only one interpretation: I was blind to what I was seeking, the Something-Other-Than that I'd spent years yearning for. In the process of my spiritual search, I was constantly losing touch with my personal identity. What was I doing wrong? My unconscious was reluctant to give me an answer.

Twenty years later, it's difficult to articulate the effect dream analysis had on my psyche and spiritual quest. During my four years of dreamwork, I don't recall any breakthrough in understanding myself or my unconscious. While I still believe in the importance of dreams, I can't point to any specific change in my actions or thinking caused by having studied them. The more I reviewed my dreams, the more confused I became about what they were trying to convey to my consciousness. Their ultimate benefit was hard to pin down. Occasionally I would think that maybe the skeptics were right; maybe dreams were mere leftovers from the day's events, reheated, and churned into a stew of images and actions, signifying nothing.

Despite my doubts, I reminded myself how Jung had been assailed by similar ones as he confronted his unconscious through his dreams. Why, Jung asked himself, was he spending so much time on such trivial matters? What did this have to do with science, his chosen field? Yet he persevered and produced monumental theories about how the human psyche works. In his book *Man and His Symbols*,[36] Jung firmly rejects the viewpoint of dreams as mental trash cans. He maintains that dreams form a bridge between the rational world of consciousness and the world of instinct, in the process attempting to restore our psychic equilibrium by producing dream material which we need to consider and pay attention to.

I find it amusing today to think back on the last dream I brought to Ron for analysis. It featured the Hollywood actor Brad Pitt as my leading man. In the dream I'm on a date with him. He complains about being bothered by the paparazzi. He kisses me, and the paparazzi take our picture. I flee both Brad and the paparazzi, wearing a coat jacket over my head. Later I brag to my family and friends about my relationship with such a big movie star. In the "real world" I wasn't a big fan of Brad Pitt, so why did he feature in my dream? Was he a stand-in for some grand passion in my life? Or a recognition of a strong male force (the animus) in my psyche? Or maybe Brad Pitt was just being "Brad Pitt." Sometimes a cigar is just a cigar.

I certainly can't claim to have made an original breakthrough in understanding my psyche through my dreams. Still, I believe analyzing my dreams stirred up my unconscious, especially during the first two years. My session notes register periods of depression, problems with stomach upsets, and skin eruptions, all physical symptoms often associated with manifestation of the unconscious. Also, for the first time in our marriage I experienced an emotional disconnect between me and my husband. My notes at the time record a remoteness totally unlike his usual self. Ron kept urging me to talk with Fraser and clear the air. I resisted the suggestion, as I couldn't articulate what, if anything, needed to be changed in our relationship. The few times I had ventured into this sensitive territory, even on

---

36. C. G. Jung, *Man and His Symbols* (New York: Bantam Books, 2023).

smaller issues, Fraser refused to acknowledge a problem existed and left me feeling like a neurotic obsessing over non-existent issues. Perhaps my husband's detachment was triggered by my dreamwork with Ron, where I might be sharing our personal issues with a stranger; or perhaps it was the financial problems experienced while he restructured his career. I can't say for sure, but I can say that after I left the dreamwork, the equilibrium in our relationship returned. If it weren't for the notes I kept of the sessions, I wouldn't know this temporary estrangement had happened. It's painful to read my notes today. I'm glad I don't remember.

By the time I left dream analysis, my periods of depression had evaporated for the most part. My difficulty dealing with my mother's emotional crisis remained unresolved. There was no solution available to me. My emotional core felt stronger and not so easily knocked off balance by her unhappiness. In some ways I had transcended the problem; in some ways the effects are with me still.

Ron felt our sessions had made me better able to use my consciousness to control my mood swings. For my part, I was disappointed not to have entertained a peak experience that laid out an overall vision of my life and its place within the vastness of humanity. But I acknowledged to myself that my expectations of dream analysis were too high. I had always felt the need to change myself to make myself more worthy in my own eyes or in the eyes of others. Then I had an epiphany of sorts: the essence of who I was at the age of five still existed inside me despite all I had learned and studied and experienced in the intervening decades. My centre, what Jung would have called the Self, felt more solid now and capable of holding me together during difficult times. When I look at photographs of myself as a young child, I'm overcome with affection, might I even say love, for this young soul. I think many of us are always striving to better ourselves, to hide our perceived faults. The flood of self-help books is testimony to this constant striving to be Something-Other-Than. I've come to believe that accepting who we are and acting from that strong centre is the way to move through the years without falling into pits of anger, depression, or guilt.

Today, almost twenty years after the conclusion of my dreamwork, I still can't identify an overarching pattern or meaning to my dreams. In reviewing my dream log and analytic notes, I'm amazed at the imagery produced by my dreams and in my active imagination. I still marvel at the genuine, enticing mystery of dreams. Such a powerful force that we are powerless to control. Where do these elaborate inner dramas we call dreams originate? Why does our body and mind produce such epics? How can I ignore this significant, albeit invisible, part of my existence?

If the unconscious has such a strong influence on my life, I want to know its face and what it has to say to me. But dreams aren't quick to give up their secrets. Despite their inscrutable nature, I respect my dreams and consider them a vital part of my being. Paying attention to them keeps me open to the invisible world of the spirit. I don't understand their significance, but I'm willing to sit in their mystery without striving frantically for meaning.

SEVEN:

THE SPIRAL

SEVEN:

THE SPIRAL

Much as I try to avoid the topic, writing a spiritual memoir requires me to face the twin horrors of the human condition—death and the afterlife. After all, it's these two dark shadows which drive us to seek a meaning to our lives. From where we sit, death cuts off our unique identity and separates us from the circle of friends and loved ones who, in so many ways, defined our years on Earth. *How can the world go on without me*, we cry out in our souls, *without the mixture of passions, abilities, and soulful insights I bring to the world?* It's extremely difficult to hold this thought for more than a few moments at a time before an existential panic begins to rise in the heart region. At that point, I usually go for a walk or raid the refrigerator for a soothing snack, my inner child reassuring me—*I eat, therefore I am.*

Before death cuts off our link to earthly existence, the body and the soul start the process of going their separate ways. This spiral of events can happen at any point, but usually starts to give off telltale signs after the age of fifty. The body and its companion mind become susceptible to an array of diseases and accidents that renders people a shadow of their former selves. There they sit, waiting for our vulnerable moment: a ghastly lineup of cell mutations, viruses, infections; confrontations with speeding planes, trains, automobiles; inundation by water and consummation by walls of smoke and fire. Cutting a life short by a bullet, a drug overdose, or the jagged edge of a knife raises the horror stakes, especially when self-administered in the manner of suicide, the most confounding yet oddly understandable death of all. So far, my body has endured attacks by cancer, diabetes, fibromyalgia, and arthritis, but still it fights on. This poem expresses my view on the outcome of this momentous struggle:

Without Which Nothing

My body, my touchstone,
my lover, my world.

I dress you in silks
from Hong Kong,
warm you with cashmere and furs.

I adorn you
with ivory and jade,
anoint you
with perfumes and cream.

I nourish your sinew
with apples and meat,
feed you only
the brownest of breads.

I sun you, I bathe you,
I breed you, I nurse you,

my child, my sorrow,
my ultimate loss
in the end.[37]

---

37. Cassidy, *Inland Waterways*, 51.

I share with millions of others a deep human fear of death, the point of non-existence our minds cannot bear to confront. Sometimes in my more mellow moods I convince myself that I've come to accept the end-of-life situation with equanimity. This is the way human existence plays out; there is no way around it. Don't waste the joys of the present with a fruitless struggle over an eternal future you are destined to lose. And for a while I think I have assented to this existential mandate. Then I witness close-up the rupture in the fabric of human existence caused by the death of a person. My stomach churns and I flee the scene.

I have avoided seeing the bodies of my grandmother, my father, and my mother, unable to endure the thought of what changes death might have inflicted on those bodies now turned into corpses. Inadvertently, I once caught sight of my uncle's body in a funeral parlour, not realizing it was an open casket service. The pool of stillness enveloping his corpse, the marble whiteness of his face left me at a loss to express an emotion or say a word. How could a previously laughing, crying, walking, running person be reduced to such an eerie stillness? Tears seemed so inadequate to the bizarre and terrifying circumstance.

Whenever I hear of the death of an acquaintance or a public figure, the first question I say to myself is "How did he or she die?" as though the answer will somehow take away the sting and put everything to rights. Other societies and cultures are far more accepting of death than the one I inhabit. They put their grief and terror on show, weeping and wailing at funeral ceremonies and parading the corpses of their loved ones in the public square. In some Eastern traditions, it's the custom to build a funeral pyre and watch the bodies of loved ones be consumed by flames while the community chants and prays with the bereaved at the grave's edge. In the West we hide this spectacle behind the curtains of the crematoria as music plays softly at a respectful level.

Except for my grandmother's death when I was ten, I was able to hunker down in my pleasant world and ignore death for over thirty years. I graduated high school, completed two degrees at university, married, and had two children; death was nowhere to be seen except in newspaper and TV accounts, background noise to my busy and important life. Finally, a heart attack opened the door, and death entered our family's life.

In 1979, two years into his retirement, it was my father's time to die. My mother and I sat in the coroner's office in Montreal and considered whether to view his body. Best not to look, we decided, at what death could do to the beloved. Outside the office, I looked back at the multi-storey building where we had left my father's body behind. A strong, primeval urge seized me—I must go back for Daddy, bring him home where we could wash his body, wrap it in fresh clothing, and lay him out in the living room of the condominium where he and my mother lived. "Don't be so silly," an inner voice echoed in my head. A second voice contradicted the first one. "But our ancestors did that all the time. It was the custom." The first practical voice prevailed, cutting off further consideration with the words, "It's unthinkable, unworkable, impossible." I turned away and walked with my mother back to the condominium.

My father's funeral was the first death ritual I had witnessed. No longer a member of the Roman Catholic Church, my father wasn't entitled to receive a funeral mass in which his casket would be blessed with holy water and incense, and the priest would offer up bread and wine. No one in my family belonged to a church, and we hadn't given thought to what would happen when death afflicted one of us. What rituals could we use to see my father off to the afterlife? We were put in touch with a

Protestant minister, who interviewed me and my mother and skillfully wove the circumstances of my father's life into what sounded like a personal eulogy. The minister read the eulogy. As the directly bereaved, custom dictated my mother and I were not to read the eulogy ourselves.

After the ceremony came the reception in the church hall— very sociable, with good food and condolences. Life and death commingled in the muted conversations amongst the bereaved, but I never heard mention of the words God, soul, or eternity. I had been dropped inside an alien land with no idea how to react. I didn't belong here. I wanted to flee.

A year later when I was sitting in a barn at the ashram in the Blue Mountains of Pennsylvania, my father's spirit presented itself in a poem, and my tears finally flowed:

Resurrection

Daddy has risen here today,
Moon shaped, sun blessed,
Blue water lights in his eyes.

He left us last year,
Not yet old, more than young,
Exploding across the black parquet,
Telephone in his hand
And his heart in shreds.

Daddy has risen here today.
A second coming was not foretold.
Not an elegant spot for revelations,
this Blue Mountain barn,
where cattle strain at their tether
and mice nibble anxiously
on grey fingernails.

His talk is no old thing.
Not a line about coal tar
That sticks in the pipes,
Or snooker with Fergie
At a nickel a drop.
Not a word about wood shots
that err to the right,
or martinis with Helen
at a quarter to seven.

No syllable stammers
the way it had felt—
extinction at sixty
before the last word.

His talk is a new thing,
His words are a smile,
His sound is a smile
A crescent, a circle,
A ring within rings
He takes everything in.[38]

With my father's passing, I woke up to the precarious nature of existence and how our perceived place in the web of world circumstance can change in a flash. A year later I created a poem to express the new-found apprehension that had penetrated my consciousness:

A Skeleton Sleeps

A skeleton sleeps in the funhouse tonight.
No one has seen him, but I know that he's there

---

38. Linda Cassidy, 1983 [unpublished].

curled under the bed with the slippers and air.

He never speaks, he never explains,
but he frightens the old, makes a blur of their sight.
He sleeps and sleeps, then suddenly scores
with a cold-handed sweep of the carpeted floors.

But we're young and we're bold, and we've got time
on our side. So close the door quickly, come quietly
down. Watch your step on the landing. It's old
and it creaks.

The fire burns brightly in the funhouse tonight.
The stereo sings and the Mozart delights.
The wine's been poured, a fine vintage red
from Château Margaux. The guests are arriving,
the fun has begun. Have you been here before?

Oh my, how divine the house looks tonight!
with the throw of the light on the emperor shag
and the print by Picasso above the black chair.
The Rosenthal vase has an elegant flair
and the couch is so lovely, all velvet and orange,
and books upon books, not a one of them bores.

Let's sit by the fire and have a bit of a treat.
Oysters on toast make an elegant feast.
I can't seem to recall, have we been here before?

A skeleton sleeps in the funhouse tonight.
No one has seen him, but I know that he's there
Curled under the bed with the slippers and air.[39]

---

39. Linda Cassidy, 1984 [unpublished].

A belief in a life after death sustains humanity in the face of what seems to be extinction in mid-breath. The possible existence of an afterlife fends off what can turn into a paralytic state of despair. A life after death offers up hope that our essence, our soul, continues to exist after the death of the body and passes over into an eternal world filled with those we have loved in life. Once the hard part of dying—the illness, the physical violence to the body, the pain—is finished, we step over a threshold into a gentler, kinder world of plenty. The existential terror of death is no more. Instead, we live in an eternity of peace.

How I wish I could attain that state of belief, or even better, that state of direct knowledge. Recently, I attended the funeral of a man whose friend testified in his eulogy that the deceased firmly believed he would sit at the feet of Jesus when he died. I marvelled at what reassurance such a belief must have given this man during his life and at his death, which I heard was a long and hard one to endure. While I envied him his peace of mind, I wouldn't want to settle for something that I hadn't known myself with certainty. Perhaps this man did have a direct experience of the divine, which made him certain in his belief in the afterlife. In which case, he was certainly a blessed man.

It seems obvious to me that the need for such reassurance is the reason humanity has created religions and gone on quests for spiritual enlightenment. The physical world of our cave ancestors must have been a frightening and harsh place to survive in. During their hunting and gathering activities they created a worldview that comforted them. Strangely, having drawn up this comforting concept of an afterlife, they came up with terrifying narratives of what happened on their arrival in this promised land. In most religions, the newly dead are submitted to a process of judgement and atonement for their actions during their lifetime. A supreme deity sits as judge, usually a personage who has conversed directly with an even more supreme deity known by various names, like God, Allah, or Osiris, the Egyptian God of the Afterlife. Those souls deemed by the supreme deity to have lived in accordance with the edicts for the faithful will be rewarded with a heavenly afterlife; those who stray from the religious directives will be dispatched to a brutish hell or vaporized into nothingness. These theologies do little to allay the fear of death.

It's fascinating to read humankind's earliest attempts to instruct people on how to enter the Land of the Dead. The two texts best known in the West are *The Tibetan Book of the Dead*[40] and *The Egyptian Book of the Dead*.[41] These texts envision the souls of the dead journeying through an interim region to an underworld filled with terrifying figures of demonic gods (both peaceful and wrathful) and hostile, dangerous animals like alligators, tigers, vultures, scorpions, and bats who drink blood and eat the entrails of corpses. *The Egyptian Book of the Dead* adds physical obstacles on the journey to the afterlife, such as lakes of fire, vast caverns, and demon creatures armed with enormous knives who guard the many gateways throughout the netherworld. To protect themselves against these terrors, the ancient Egyptians compiled a collection of individual sheets of papyrus inscribed with hieroglyphics of magic spells, rituals, ancient texts, and prayers, which were placed inside and outside the sarcophagi and inscribed on tomb walls.

The intent of both these books of the dead was to attain a favourable reincarnation and ultimate liberation of the soul from the wheel of existence. In a commentary prepared by Jung for a contemporary Western audience, he likened these regions

40. *Tibetan Book of the Dead*, compiled and edited by W. Y. Evans-Wentz (Oxford: Oxford University Press, 1980).

41. Wallis Budge, *The Egyptian Book of the Dead* (Mineola, N.Y.: Dover Publications, Inc., 2012).

of torment to various states of psychic consciousness. For Jung, the teachings in these ancient scriptures confirmed his view of the primacy of the soul as the radiant Godhead itself, which lies within us all and functions as an extension of the collective unconscious.

In the *Egyptian Book of the Dead* there is a particularly gruesome scene of judgement where a tribunal of forty-two deities weighs the heart of the deceased on a scale against the goddess of truth and justice, represented by an ostrich feather. If the scales balance, this signifies the deceased has led a good life and is entitled to spend eternity working the fields—considered a heavenly pursuit, I presume, by the Egyptians of that day. On the other hand, if the scales do not balance, the deceased are handed over to a fearsome beast who stands ready to eat the damned, putting a quick end to their time in this heavenly place.

To avoid the fate of eternal damnation, every religion offers up its own version of rituals, prayers, and theologies for the faithful to perform during their time on Earth. This promise of salvation attracts millions of believers to their faith and to the execution of deeds of great love and great evil in the name of that faith and its supreme deity. This carrot-and-stick approach to religious salvation strikes me as inherently cruel and overly simplistic. The approach is modelled on the schoolroom, an environment familiar to most every person on the planet, where students dutifully learn their lessons from a strict teacher, pass exams on what they have learned, and hopefully are rewarded for their success with a sticker of a bright red robin or a blue rose. If some form of afterlife exists, I suspect something much more complex is at play than simply punishment for our misbehaviour.

It's understandable that our human imagination would fail at the task of envisioning an afterlife where our soul operates without a physical body in a world governed by utterly different sets of rules. We're getting a glimpse of how these different rules might appear to us in the recent revolutionary theories in the scientific field of physics. A few of these theories, like quantum mechanics, superstring theory, and general relativity, are already modifying our understanding of space, time, and matter. I can foresee the day when these revelations might well expand our understanding of what happens to us after we die in a way that transcends traditional religious teachings. Physics is a powerful tool because it deals with the invisible world not available to the human senses. Spiritual seekers of the future will need to take such developments into account. And science will need to take into account human insights into what it takes to live in such an evidence-based world.

Evidence of an afterlife has been described in accounts of near-death experiences put forth by patients who have medically "died" while on the operating table. They speak of having passed through a world of light filled with images of dead friends and family, only to be told it wasn't their time and they must return to the everyday plane of existence. Most are reluctant to return. While interesting to read, these accounts brought out the skeptic in me. I didn't want to have to nearly die to confirm if my loved ones would be there to meet me in the afterlife.

Then I discovered Jung's typically unique view on the matter. In *Memories, Dreams, Reflections*, Jung spends an entire chapter candidly presenting his views on the afterlife. He acknowledges that anything he might have to say about death and the hereafter is sheer conjecture on his part, and he could never prove his case with legal precision. Nevertheless, he underscores how human beings still yearn with an overwhelming intensity for a reason to believe that their spirit, if not their body, goes on after we die. The question of immortality is so urgent for humanity and so immediate, Jung considered it a healing and valid emotional activity to spend time thinking about life after death, even if we can't know whether our thoughts are true or not.

Jung advises us not to approach the question of immortality as an intellectual or scientific problem because we will never know the answer with any degree of certainty. The language related to eternity is not couched in the language of the intellect. Instead, he recommends turning to the hints of immortality given us by the unconscious through our dream images and incidents of parapsychology, precognition, and synchronistic phenomena. Using these meagre clues, Jung suggests we build our own myth of life after death.

Whether or not anyone else believes in our personal myth is of little consequence, as long as it's meaningful and believable to us. In his view, relying solely on a reasonable, provable view of the afterlife can lead a person on a long march toward a dark pit of nothingness, causing him or her to become embittered against an unmerciful, unkind God. A positive vision of the afterlife taken in accordance with an individual's personal beliefs makes his or her current life more enjoyable and healthier. Based on the inner promptings from his unconscious, Jung formed his own view of the afterlife, which he found comforting and rewarding.

While Jung conceded the fearful wantonness and brutality of death, he also spoke of a certain joyfulness in death when the soul attains its missing half and achieves a wholeness. Late in his life, Jung almost died in the aftermath of a heart attack. During an early stage in the death process, a great joy enveloped him, and he experienced amazing and joyous visions.

I like Jung's personal take on the afterlife: *It is what you believe it to be.* Many would consider this an untenable, unsatisfactory non-answer. Given our current inability to prove anyone's vision the "correct" one, I consider it's the only answer possible for the singular person seeking a direct experience of the Truth. I think back upon the oft-quoted advice given by Rilke to a struggling young poet who bombarded him with questions about the universe and the practice of poetry. His advice to the young man given in 1903 seems applicable over a hundred years later to my questions about the afterlife:

> I want to beg you, as much as I can, dear sir, to be patient toward all that is unsolved in your heart and try to love the questions themselves like locked rooms and like books that are written in a very foreign tongue. Do not now seek the answers, which cannot be given you because you would not be able to live them. And the point is, to live everything. Live the questions now. Perhaps you will then gradually, without noticing it, live along some distant day into the answer.[42]

Like Rilke's young poet friend, I am seeking an answer to a question that can't be given because no one can lay claim to knowing the answer. If someone does make such a claim, I would know immediately I was in the presence of a charlatan looking to fleece me of my worldly wealth. The only way to find the answer to the question of the afterlife is to live the question in hope that one day the answer will be revealed before I pass over into the world of Something-Other-Than.

A medieval Christian text written by a friar provides an image and name for the current state of my quest and my spirit. This mystical work, referred to as *The Cloud of Unknowing*,[43] postulates that God is unknowable and cannot be understood by

---

42. Rainier Maria Rilke, *Letters to a Young Poet*, trans. Stephen Mitchell (New York: Random House, 1984).

43. *The Cloud of Unknowing [and other works]*, trans. Clifton Wolters (New York: Penguin Books, 1961).

the human intellect. Faced with such an unknowable God, the conscious mind seizes up, becomes blank, and enters a cloud of unknowing. I stand now under a Cloud of Unknowing, waiting for the cloud to move on and reveal the clear blue vault of the sky. Someday, I may step into that sunlit place, where I will finally find that Something-Other-Than. Or maybe I won't know until death kindly stops for me and shows me the way.

EIGHT:

ENDPOINT

EIGHT:

ENDPOINT

For life's a shabbybody subterfuge,
And death is real, and dark, and huge.[44]

From the chair at the foot of my husband's bed, I can see his face clearly. His expression is relaxed—no struggle, no visible doubt or fear about the decision he's taken. He has nothing to say to us. We are past words, beyond the gravitational pull of relationships, even the sacred ones of husband and father. He appears happy. I even sense in him a frisson of anticipation. Not strange, for at heart my husband is an explorer, keen to probe the physical world, especially rivers, great lakes, and blue water seas. I know his voyager heart is looking forward to this final terrifying yet amazing voyage of his lifetime. But for those of us about to be left behind on this earthly dock, we are not relaxed or at peace. A husband and a father are being torn out of the fabric of our lives, leaving for a destination from which he can never return to us.

---

44. John Updike, "Requiem," in *Endpoint and Other Poems* (New York: Knopf, 2009). 93

The doctor sits on the bed, holding the syringe in his hand. Two nurses remain near the door to his hospital room, witnesses to this modern ritual of death, where the human sacrifice invites the executioner to his bedside.

"Do I have your permission," the doctor asks, "to give you this injection?"

"Yes," my husband replies without hesitation. My heart pounds hard against my ribcage.

The doctor makes a small forward movement, holds the position for a moment, and then sits back upright. I watch my husband's face transform. His eyes are open and aware, soft brown and kindly, the man I knew; then the eyes are hard as marble, glassy, unmoving. He is gone. The spirit that made him who he was, it has vanished.

The doctor looks at the clock on the wall; "10:25," he tells the nurses. He unwraps the rubber band from around my husband's limp arm. The nurse scribbles in her notebook. The doctor turns and speaks to me and my sons. I don't recall his words. Condolences, I expect, for the doctor is a compassionate man who frees the souls of those trapped inside the coffin of a pain-wracked, dying body.

The medical observers quietly leave the room. I stand up and embrace my sons. We weep. Nothing more to say. We are locked inside a silence where words dissolve before they reach the tongue. We move around the end of the bed toward the door. I turn back for a last look. The florescent light from the ceiling bathes the hospital room in a shadowless, dazzling whiteness. The top of my husband's skull shines, and his toes poke out from underneath the blanket. I wish him a soft landing wherever the Eternal takes him. The bars on the side of the hospital bed prevent me from bending down to kiss his cheek. That's all right. He's already left the room.

The house is quiet, nothing to be heard except the hum of the refrigerator and the whoosh of cool air from the air-conditioning vent. An hour ago, I breakfasted on cereal and cream sprinkled with plump blueberries and brown sugar, followed by the ten multicoloured pills I take every day to keep my soul from escaping my body. Then a ten-minute walk around the block and fifteen minutes watering the lawn, hoping the newly scattered seeds will germinate. Before I head to my study for a two-hour bout of writing, I stretch my body in many directions for fifteen minutes and slip in a few exercises in hopes of easing the discomfort in bone and muscle. My body does not appreciate the attention. Ungrateful creature.

Over the last few months, I've noticed a tendency to carve my days up into minutes and hours. In the morning, two hours are spent at the keyboard hammering out the next chapter in my current writing project, then lunch from 1:00 p.m. to 2:00 p.m., followed by a blessed nap preceded by a quick read of a popular mystery story. Gardening chores fill a couple of hours in the afternoon. Working in the garden, once a supreme delight, is now blighted with arthritic feet and legs and back, but I can't let go of working in the soil, a source of primal delight for so many years. I'm on my fourth garden, which will be my last one. The dandelions have been particularly vigorous this spring, their astonishing yellowness so beautiful but so unwanted in a gardener's vision of the perfect green lawn. Those weeds from hell don't care a fig if my body hurts. They continue to flaunt their yellow blooms that eventually will turn light grey and feathery and fly away to propagate more dandelions in the neighbourhood.

Dinner in front of the television happens around 7:00 p.m., give or take half an hour. As the only diner, I have the luxury of picking and choosing my moment to dine. My dining companions come from the world of television, most often the anchors on the multiple news channels. One worldly disaster after the other. Too much, too violent to bear alone. I look over at Fraser's empty chair to share my exasperation about how the world's population can't seem to stop harming itself with rapacious dictators, torture, starvation, bullets, and roadside bombs. Not being one who can converse with the dead, even in my imagination, I switch channels, seeking a skillful drama or detective series, hopefully one without scenes at the morgue where the detectives peer at the fatal wounds of the corpse. I could read a book, of course, but I have spent much of my day reading and writing. By the evening I'm mentally fatigued and prefer to be entertained and inspired by others. The day closes at 11:00 p.m., give or take an hour, with a spot of easy, neutral reading. I need to be careful about what I read before bedtime. New ideas supercharge my mind and can chase sleep away for hours.

These days my calendar overflows with appointments with doctors, dentists, and pharmacists—the medical team required to keep my body and soul working in tandem. Like everyone else in Toronto, my social circle has shrunk; a worldwide plague has driven humanity indoors to escape its ravages. The sick, the dying, and the dead have overwhelmed the hospitals and mortuaries. Pandemics show no mercy.

My spiritual quest has struck two colossal bumps along the road to enlightenment—the death of my life partner and advancing old age. Increasingly, the infirmities that come with entering my eighth decade are slowing me down both physically and mentally. I still read and write but not with the energy and creative ferocity of even two years ago. I'm no longer expecting the Big Bang of a religious conversion where the voice of God speaks to me or the universal sea parts to reveal the way forward for me and my tribe.

From time to time, I speculate about what will happen to me when I die. I envision possible scenarios, but I feel like a blind person peering through a keyhole. I don't go to that place in my mind very often. Why rush it? One day I'll find out the truth for myself. I'm in line with the wish of the Canadian poet-songwriter Leonard Cohen, who was quoted shortly before his death, "I hope it doesn't hurt too much." Unfortunately, I won't be able to come back to this earthly realm and brag about my divine knowledge. If a profound change in the laws of the universe were to permit such an event, it's highly unlikely anyone will believe me. And that's fine with me. I wouldn't want millions of faithful followers initiating unholy wars and crusades in my name and murdering thousands of people to convince everyone of the truth proclaimed in my words. I would prefer to say nothing and let others discover their own truth.

My few encounters with what I consider to be a hint of the divine have never manifested as a human image or voice, either male or female or anything in between. The accounts of sages and men of deep faith often include more human features in their visions, especially the holiest ones who founded great religions. Instead, this Something-Other-Than feels to me less a person, and more like an energy force that moves through my body of its own accord, bringing with it a delightfully sweet sensation of transcendental love and being at peace with myself and my world. Perhaps this same life force inhabits every plant, bird, fish, animal, and human on the planet, making up the source of all existence. Perhaps it's the source of all life. Perhaps after death my spirit soul will rejoin this vast matrix of soulful beings. Perhaps ... perhaps ... perhaps. The uncertainty and the questions keep on coming. I struggle to remain calm and live on in Keats's state of "negative capability," comfortable in the midst of uncertainty, mystery, and doubt.

Despite my newly found patience in waiting for the answer to the mystery of human existence, pockets of rage still burn inside my psyche. Why am I and my fellow humans barred from knowing the reason and ultimate purpose for the great suffering in the world? Where does compassion and relief for our human species lie? How long are we to remain bound together on this exquisite blue planet in a web of good and evil and remain ignorant of the endpoint of our cosmic travels? We appear destined to hurtle in ignorance through a dark, cold space interspersed with galaxies of gaseous stars and exploding supernovas in a universe created on a scale that dwarfs our feeble dreams and desires.

Christian theology claims that we have no control over whether we can touch, see, or speak with the divine. In their view, it all comes down to a matter of grace, a spontaneous, undeserved favour from God. Until this mysterious and unpredictable grace reveals the divine to me, I intend to carry on to the endpoint with poetry and see what unfolds along the way.

NINE:

THE WAY OF THE COSMOS

NINE:
THE WAY OF THE COSMOS

I wish I were able to conclude this memoir with an account of my transition into the afterlife, if such there be, and my return wrapped in the bliss of enlightenment and ready to speak the truths revealed to me along the way. What a spiritual news scoop of transcendental proportions that would be! However, the laws of nature and the spirit world cannot be overridden. At this stage in our human evolution, I can only stand here and see where I have landed. Where have my years of seeking for that Something-Other-Than brought me?

Pelican Lost

deep in the Arctic snow
far from the coast
the pelican is in a strange land
her deep, orange pouch empty
of the frogs and salamanders
she loves to eat
she wonders how she got here

did she read the wrong guidebooks
perhaps she should have studied

maps more closely, ones that show
clearly where she should nest
where she might find like-minded creatures
with deep full beaks, a passion for loving
and an aversion to cold weather[45]

I may have been premature in concluding my spiritual journey has ended. Yes, I remain a bit of a lost soul still, yearning still for that something I cannot name. But, I strongly feel the journey hasn't been wasted. The added ability to touch the edge of the ineffable Something-Other-Than through poetry remains for me the gift of a lifetime. Poetry will continue to be my spiritual north star to the endpoint of my existence.

Despite my claim to be at the endpoint of my quest, I find myself drawn to yet another way to continue the journey. I've named this alternate path, "The Way of the Cosmos."

In 1957, humanity began to physically explore the metaphorical heavens to see what really existed there. That year the Russians launched *Sputnik I*, the first artificial Earth satellite. I was in my last year of high school and vividly recall the excitement fermented by this breakthrough event. The graduation photo in my 1958 high school yearbook notes my ambition was to be a Canadian ambassador to Russia, and my probable destiny was to be ejected into space in *Sputnik III*. Over the next six decades, a parade of astronomical achievements included a man on the moon, an international space station, more and more powerful space telescopes, and frequent rocket launches to other planets in the Earth's Milky Way galaxy.

All this activity has revealed more and more mind-bending information about the physical origins and evolution of our universe. Heaven is no longer just an arc of overhead sky—blue in the

---

45. Cassidy, *Inland Waterways*, 44.

daytime with shifting layers of cloud where angels sit and play the harp, or black at nighttime with points of starlight suggesting God's eyes. The human horizon is being stretched beyond a thumbnail view of the heavens to include worlds beyond worlds, spinning in clusters of stars at distances beyond our imaginings and technical capabilities to access. Whether this new learning will bring human-kind closer to knowing more about the life of the spirit, about how to connect with that Something-Other-Than, we don't know yet. All I know is that we share a limitless universe with galactic worlds of light and dark, dust and rock and winds. They exist, we exist, we were once a part of each other, a singularity together. We need to explore it.

After graduating from university, the demands of my earth-bound life pushed aside the early attraction I'd felt for space exploration. Recent advances in astronomy, physics, and cos-mology have restored my interest in space. In the early 2020s, more powerful telescopes, like the Hubble Space Telescope (launched in 1990) and the James Webb Space Telescope (launched in 2021), have revealed never-before-seen high-resolution photographs of the stars and galaxies in outer space. At the same time, space travel and electronic monitoring for intelligent beings on other planets are no longer limited to the imagination of science fiction writers but have become a repu-table arena for scientific research. Plans to put a man on the moon are once again on NASA's planning board for 2025.

We are getting to know more and more about the vastness of the world in which we find ourselves embedded. Photographs taken from satellites show planet Earth as a small blue dot in black space orbiting a star-sun within a mammoth cluster of billions of stars called the Milky Way galaxy, which itself is only one galaxy of millions. The universe is a violent place. Radiation, dust, gases, and gigantic rocks travel at colossal speeds, frequently colliding with each other, while dying stars explode into supernovas with a luminosity a billion times that of the sun. Earth is protected from these forces of chaos by the thinnest film of oxygenated atmospheres, our current blue heaven. We have no sense of this world of violence. We sit on the patio behind a glass darkly as we sip our glass of lemonade on a sunny afternoon.

Sun Stroke

I sit on the lawn chair, eyes closed,
the sun so warm and tender. Its shimmering
light freckles my pale winter skin
and soothes my hyperactive mind.
I don't dare gaze directly at this fiery sphere
of hydrogen and helium which is the sun.
Its glare can blur my vision and threaten
me with cataracts and forever blindness.

Astronomers, those scholars of the skies,
tell us the sun's rotating sphere releases
blasts of nuclear energy from its core,
throwing out jets of gaseous heat
into the airless void of space
at temperatures so extreme as to defy
all attempts at personal reckoning.

The sun doesn't appear that far away,
a mere eight minutes, the astronomers say.
But these scientific folk speak a foreign dialect
of measurement rooted in the speed of light,
a blend of time and space. Distance from Earth
to sun ninety-one million miles: by family car
it takes 177 years; by jet a mere twenty years.
Round trip tickets can take a lifetime to use.

Passing through a prairie inscape of darkest dark
and coldest cold, the solar inferno comes
to rest gently on my bare arms and legs
giving me the gift of a perfect summer tan.
Were I to travel this same route, unprotected
by a NASA space suit or a rocket ship, I
would die in the space of a single breath.

Since lunch I've travelled millions of miles
through space, yet never encountered
its perishing cold or been scarred
by the perpetual darkness, or gasped
my last breath. Protected by the sanctuary
of Planet Earth, I'm able to swim,
sunbathe, and drink cool lemonade.

In a few hours, this blazing sphere will roll
across the treetops and drop out of sight.
Darkness will consume everything. Tomorrow,
the sun will rise on the far side of the lake and
the twin miracles of warmth and light will spread
once more across the land. Eternal renewal.

Everything will look the same to me,
where I sit by the white sandy beach
lapped by blue waters, a cloudless sky,
even the cool wet glass in my hand.

Nothing has changed
and yet since lunch,
everything has changed.[46]

---

46. Linda Cassidy, 2023 [unpublished].

The discoveries arising from space exploration have, for many of us, shaken our confidence in what we thought we knew about our universe, both inner and outer. By outer space is meant external, physical happenings, while inner space refers to the psychological and metaphysical import assigned to these facts by the human mind and spirit. A revelation can arise from inner space and meet up with impressions brought by the senses from outer space to the mind. Sometimes this convergence of dissimilar realities will find a mutual synthesis that can cause inner and outer space to be merged and absorbed into a single organic whole, called a myth or a religion.

Joseph Campbell has written extensively about the relationship between inner and outer space and its effect on mythologies both folk and religious. He has been quoted as saying the laws of space are within us, and therefore outer space and inner space are the same. He paints outer space as a magnificent creation of "unimaginable magnitude and inconceivable violence: billions upon billions—literally—of roaring thermonuclear furnaces (stars) scattering away from each other."[47]

Campbell cites an early medieval text that states, "God is an infinite sphere, whose centre is everywhere and circumference nowhere."[48] This early statement of the essence of God was made before telescopes and rockets were even a concept in anyone's mind. Today's powerful telescopes reveal the cosmos filled with a million spinning galaxies, each with billions of stars, all moving at prodigious rates away from each other and with no still point anywhere.

In the face of these new revelations, Campbell asked a difficult and pertinent question. What is to happen in mythological terms now that "the old gods are dead or dying and people everywhere

---

47. Joseph Campbell, *The Inner Reaches of Outer Space: Metaphor as Myth and as Religion* (Novato, California: New World Library, 2002), 2.

48. Campbell, *The Inner Reaches of Outer Space*, 18.

are searching, asking: What is the new mythology to be, the mythology of this unified Earth as of one harmonious being?"[49] Obviously, he claims, some corrections to our inner space thinking about myths and religion need to be made. In the 1980s he was already pointing out how humankind needs to adjust their inner psyche to align with the new celestial truths coming into view. Can a more extensive knowledge of outer space provide us with a better, more truthful way to find a meaning and spiritual understanding in our world? I would love the chance to find out, but I must bow to the limited human lifespan.

Many people today, including myself, are caught in the no-man's-land between the observations and theories of modern science and the ancient spiritual renderings of the universe as documented in sacred texts. The human condition never leaves us. Given our finite lifespan, we are utterly unable to know our purpose and fate. We live on planet Earth for a flash of universal time, so short it's hard to calculate when compared to the standard space measurement of billions of light years. What exactly does it mean to grow from childhood to old age on this planet and then to depart forever, with no knowledge of our continued existence or ultimate destination? How do we live with this paralyzing conundrum?

The exploration of space over the last thirty years has made it more important than ever to connect and resolve the seemingly incompatible truths observed in inner and outer space. In grappling with this meaning, humankind will need to dig deep into the powers of its imagination and collective unconscious. Poetry is one tool that can bypass the barrier of the consciousness to reveal reality afresh. Poets, painters, and musicians have already begun to gather and consider nature, science, and astronomy in a way that will expand the common ground between the scientific and the poetic worldviews. In coming to grips with the scope of such

---

49. Campbell, *The Inner Reaches of Outer Space*, xix.

an undertaking, I found the website of an organization called The Universe in Verse very helpful. This organization celebrates the science and splendour of nature through poetry (https://www.the-marginalian.org/?s=universe+in+verse). Topics on the site include "Dreams, Consciousness, and the Nature of the Universe" and "Consciousness and the Constellation." The rethinking of a new mythology and religious theology for space has begun.

I've made a few dives into writing poems that highlight the conflicting views of inner and outer space:

Moon Show

I gaze up at the moon where it hangs
in the night air almost resting
on my neighbour's roof, a fullish moon,
oyster-white, speckled with dark craters.
This is a lover's moon, the kind poets
praise to the skies. Its lunar radiance
serves as the queen of ecstasy and
soulful intoxication.

And yet I've seen the videos
time and time again. Men housed
in space suits bouncing over the moon's
surface. No air to breathe, no lunar seas,
no rivers, forests—only dust, everywhere dust,
and craters carved out by falling meteorites
and lava flow from the moon's molten centre.

Dry, dry, everything bone-dry, like scales
on a dead dinosaur. Not life as I have ever
known it or would wish it to be.[50]

---

50. Linda Cassidy, 2022 [unpublished].

When I'm feeling emotionally and physically strong, I sometimes attempt to think long and intensely about what these discoveries in astrophysics and cosmology mean for humanity's future. The effort can set my mind spinning in multiple concentric circles, each one seemingly attempting to push the other circles aside. The more I lean forward into what this new perspective on our origins and existence may mean for future generations, the more a pressure builds across my forehead and chest, to the point where I worry my brain's neural networks may entrap themselves in a massive quantum entanglement. At this stress point, I back off and go for a walk through the streets of the here and now. I look up at the night sky and find myself wondering:

How I Wonder

Stars—those otherworldly points of light—
never do they cease to twinkle. All night long
they render cosmic light, constellations from
a genesis launched fourteen billion years ago.

We love the stars; they make us dream.
At sight of them, our hearts yearn to touch
these eyes of God as we would caress
the beauty of a loved one's face.

Stars glitter like diamond rings. Sometimes, the fates
of lovers do not align. We call them star-crossed
as though a distant point of light makes all the difference
between the loving and the fighting.

We have read the stars as scripture for our restless souls,
the place where our births and destinies arise, galactic
maps for sailors seeking harbour on a clear night,
even signs for Oriental kings searching for the Holy Child.

No longer can we wish upon a star and hope our dreams
come true. For Earth has dared to turn its telescopic eyes
on the churning grandeur of the spiral galaxies,
even launching spaceships to reach behind God's eyes.

Once fictions of our free-wheeling imagination, today
the stars are charted, measured, photographed, and analyzed.
No longer exemplars of myths and visions, but speeding
spheres of hydrogen and helium fired by nuclear explosions.

Twinkle, twinkle all night long. Oh, royal stars
of beauty bright, all those atoms, protons, neutrons
exploding in the sky. Once signifiers of our godly
yearning, divine protectors for friends and lovers,

now, oh now,
my holy ones,
I wonder what you truly are.[51]

I realize the divine has not chosen to grace me with a one-on-one encounter. So far, no personal god has spoken to me, even though I keep my pencil at the ready to take dictation with the hope that I, like the poet Rilke, might turn such a conversation into poems of divine illumination.

At this point in my search, I have the inward sensation of floating on my back in a wide stream that moves slowly through the woods toward a grand lake that eventually will empty into an endless ocean. Some days the sky is blue, and the floating is serene; other days cascades of rain and snow fall from dark clouds. Staying in the floating position on those days puts me in danger of a panic attack. Experience—many years of it—tells

---

51. Linda Cassidy, 2022 [unpublished].

me the storm will not last forever. For the moment, I am content once again, until the final storm appears on the horizon.

Several months ago, a poem arose spontaneously from my unconscious. I didn't have to edit it in any way; it manifested on my yellow legal pad in one organic piece. While the meaning of the poem eludes me, it infuses my soul with a strange surge of joy:

Something-Other-Than

Small joys can come from the dog
who jumps over the sun and falls
into a fiery ball at your feet
where he shakes the ashes
off his fur, licks your hand
and takes you for a walk.[52]

THE END

---

52. Linda Cassidy, 2021 [unpublished].

WORKS CITED

Alighieri, Dante. *The Divine Comedy.* New York: Penguin Books, 2013.

Auden, W. H. "In Memory of Ernst Toller," in *The Complete Works of W. H. Auden: Poems, vol. II 1940–1974.* Princeton, New Jersey: Princeton University Press, 2022.

Bachelard, Gaston. The Poetics of Space. Boston: Beacon Press, 1969.

Budge, Wallis. *The Egyptian Book of the Dead.* Mineola, N.Y.: Dover Publications, Inc., 2012.

Campbell, Joseph. *The Inner Reaches of Outer Space: Metaphor as Myth and as Religion.* Novato, California: New World Library, 2002.

Cassidy, Linda. Inland Waterways: Poems from a Peaceable Kingdom. Mississauga, ON: Our Words, Inc. (IOWI), 2010.

The Cloud of Unknowing [and other works]. Translated by Clifton Wolters. New York: Penguin Books, 1961.

Desai, Yogi Amrit. *Guru and Disciple: A Relationship of Love.* Sumneytown, Pa.: Kripalu Yoga Ashram, 1975.

Dickinson, Emily. *Acts of Light: Poems by Emily Dickinson* with an appreciation by Jane Langton. Boston, New York: Graphic Society, 1980.

Dickinson, Emily. *Letters of Emily Dickinson.* Edited by Mabel Loomis Todd. North Chelmsford, Mass.: Courier Corporation, 2003.

Farmer, Linda. *IRON Magazine* (1973–1997). No. 43, June 1984. North Shields, Northumberland, UK: IRON Press https://www.ironpress.co.uk/news.html.

The Holy Geeta: Commentary by Swami Chinmayananda. Bombay: Central Chinmaya Mission Trust, [n.d.].

Hillman, James. *The Dream and the Underworld.* New York: Harper and Row, 1975.

James, William. *The Varieties of Religious Experience: A Study in Human Nature.* New York: The Modern Library, 2002.

Johnson, Robert A. *Inner Work: Using Dreams & Active Imagination for Personal Growth.* New York: HarperSanFrancisco, 1986.

Jung, C. G. *Man and His Symbols.* New York: Bantam Books, 2023.

Jung, C. G. *Memories, Dreams, Reflections.* New York: Random House, 1989.

Jung, C. G. *Psychology and the East.* Princeton: Princeton University Press, 1978.

Jung, C. G. *The Red Book, Liber Novus.* New York: W. W. Norton & Company, 2009.

Krishnamurti, Jiddu. *Freedom From the Known.* London: Victor Gollancz Ltd., 1972.

Muni, Rajarshi. *Light from Guru to Disciple.* Sumneytown, Pa.: Kripalu Yoga Ashram, 1974.

The Power of the Word Project. https://poweroftheword project.com

Rajendra. *Journey to the New Age: An Introduction to Life at Kripalu Yoga Ashram.* Sumneytown, Pa.: Kripalu Yoga Fellowship, 1976.

Rilke, Rainier Maria. *Duino Elegies and The Sonnets to Orpheus.* New York: Random House, 2009.

Rilke, Rainier Maria. *Letters to a Young Poet.* Translated by Stephen Mitchell. New York: Random House, 1984.

Rilke, Rainer Maria. *Rilke's Book of Hours: Love Poems to God.* Translated by Anita Barrows and Joanna Macy. New York: Riverhead Books/Penguin Group, 2005.

Singer, June. *Boundaries of the Soul: The Practice of Jung's Psychology.* New York: Random House, 1994.

Stevens, Anthony. *Private Myths: Dreams and Dreaming.* London: Hamish Hamilton, 1995.

The Upanishads. Translated by Alistair Shearer and Peter Russell. London: Unwin Paperbacks, 1989.

Tibetan Book of the Dead. Compiled and edited by W. Y. Evans-Wentz. Oxford: Oxford University Press, 1980.

Updike, John. "Requiem" in *Endpoint and Other Poems.* New York: Knopf, 2009.

Van der Post, Laurens. *Jung and the Story of Our Time.* London: Penguin Books, 1976.

Whitman, Walt. *Leaves of Grass. The First (1855) Edition.* Edited with an introduction by Malcolm Cowley. London: Penguin Books, 1976.

Wu, Duncan, ed. *Romanticism: An Anthology.* Third Edition. Hoboken, New Jersey: Blackwell, 2006.

SUGGESTED READINGS

Many books exist in libraries and bookstores having to do with the spiritual quest. The ones listed here are just a few that I found particularly helpful. Reading these books will lead on to others just as useful and inspiring.

Armstrong, Karen. *A History of God: The 4,000-Year Quest of Judaism, Christianity and Islam.* New York: Ballantine Books, 1993.

Armstrong, Karen. *Muhammad: A Prophet for our Time*. New York: HarperOne, 2006.

Brunton, Paul. *A Hermit in the Himalayas: The Journal of a Lonely Exile*. London: Rider and Company, 1969.

Campbell, Joseph. *Pathways to Bliss: Mythology and Personal Transformation*. Novato, California: New World Library, 2004.

Kuhn, Alvin Boyd. *The Lost Light: An Interpretation of Ancient Scriptures*. Mansfield Centre, Connecticut: Martino Publishing, 2015.

Knox, Francesca Bugliani and John Took, eds. *Poetry and Prayer: The Power of the Word [Conference II]*. London: Routledge, 2015.

Raine, Kathleen. *The Inner Journey of the Poet [and other papers]*. London: George Allen & Unwin, 1982.

Song of God: Bhagavad-Gita. Translated by Swami Prabhavananda and Christopher Isherwood. New York: New American Library, 1951.

Von Franz, Marie-Louise. *Alchemy: An Introduction to the Symbolism and the Psychology*. Toronto: Inner City Books, 1980.

ABOUT THE AUTHOR

Linda Cassidy worked as a professional librarian and technical writer for many years while also exploring the spiritual aspect of life. She became a disciple of a yoga master and for eight years attended meditation workshops at a yoga ashram in Pennsylvania. She undertook dream work for four years with a Jungian analyst, all the while devoting herself to the writing of poetry. Now in her eighth decade, she shares the fruit of her research and participation in a journey of the spirit.

In 2010 Cassidy published her first book, a collection of poetry titled *Inland Waterways: Poems from a Peaceable Kingdom*, and in 2020 she published a mystery thriller, *The Long Revenge*. She's a member of The Writers' Union of Canada, the League of Canadian Poets, Crime Writers of Canada, and the Heliconian Club for women active in the arts and literature.

Cassidy has lived in Oakville, Ontario for over thirty years and now resides in downtown Toronto where she focuses on the joy of writing poetry and attending readings. She has two adult sons and two granddaughters.

Printed in the USA
CPSIA information can be obtained
at www.ICGtesting.com
LVHW092324040324
773504LV00001B/145

9 781039 175075